SOCIAL SERVICES FOR OLDER PERSONS

Albert J.E. Wilson III

Belle Boone Beard Gerontology Center
Lynchburg College

WAVELAND
PRESS, INC.
Prospect Heights, Illinois

6-8-01

For information about this book, write or call:

Waveland Press, Inc.
P.O. Box 400
Prospect Heights, Illinois 60070
(312) 634-0081

ISBN 0-88133-383-2

Printed in the United States of America

7 6 5 4 3 2 1

SOCIAL SERVICES FOR OLDER PERSONS

Preface

The decision to write this book was based on my inability to locate a suitable text for my seminars on programs for older persons and recognition that others also needed a text of this type. For me, a suitable text was one that avoided the bias of any single discipline, provided a broad view of service program structure using an "ideal type" model, included material on planning and evaluation, and related program structure to social policy and legislation. This book does not go into great depth on any one topic, but includes extensive documentation for those who do wish to pursue a given subject.

This work reflects my experiences in both agency and academic settings and strikes a middle ground between the ivory tower and community service delivery systems. It may be used as a basic or supplementary text for college and university courses, as a text for inservice training, or as a resource document.

I wish to express my appreciation to some of those who assisted with and facilitated the preparation of this manuscript. Constructive criticism by Jon Hendricks helped to shape the content and sequence of material. My wife Nera's patience and encouragement were essential to maintain motivation for the project. Julia Winston and Sally Lifland deserve special credit for their careful attention to detail and helpful suggestions during the editing process. Sincere thanks are also due to Gerre Briggs, who typed the final manuscript from edited drafts. Finally, very special recognition is given to the students with whom the material was tested. This book is dedicated to Beth, Clement, Doris, Elmond, Gloria, Jean, John, Jordon, Kay, Leslie, Marian, Nikki, Pauline, and Susan.

Contents

Chapter
1

Introduction

Community services specifically directed toward the older population in general are a relatively recent development in the United States. Early research and services concentrated on the most dependent elderly and apparently contributed to some of the misconceptions and stereotypes basic to "ageism." Although the so-called frail or vulnerable older people remain an important target population for social services, increasing attention is being directed toward the active, involved, and independent persons, who constitute a substantial majority of our older population (Tibbitts, 1977a, b). With this expansion of focus, policies have emphasized opportunities for growth and development, support services to enable older persons to maintain optimal levels of activity and independence, and programs to prevent or reduce age-related physical, psychological, and social impairments.

Definition of Older Person

Most social service programs use chronological age to define status as an "older person." Chronological age has a general, but imprecise, relationship to any individual's functional age in terms of biological, psychological, and social capacities. It is, however, useful for categorizing people for administrative purposes.

Although age 65 is widely used to define entry into old age, there is no uniform standard among social service providers. The Social Security Administration's adoption of 65 as retirement age in the

1930s resulted from a complex set of influences. A precedent had been established in Germany and other European countries at an earlier time. Although life expectancy in the United States in the 1930s was quite different from that in Germany in the 1880s, the cutoff at age 65 proved to be politically popular and functional for prevailing economic conditions.

In those countries which have public old-age pensions, age 65 commonly defines the point of withdrawal from the labor force. Thus it is used in computation of the age dependency ratio. Demographers and planners use the dependency ratio as a rough indicator of the number of potentially nonproductive persons per 100 potentially productive persons, based on age categories. The "dependent" population is divided into youth dependency (persons too young to be productive) and old-age dependency (persons too old to be productive) (Schultz, 1980; Maddox and Wiley, 1976).

Initially, the federal Older Americans Act of 1965 did not include a specific age for eligibility. Subsequent amendments adopted age 60 as the point at which one becomes an "older American." However, the senior employment programs (authorized under the Older Americans Act but transferred to the Department of Labor for administration) use age 55 in their definition of a senior worker (U.S. DHEW, 1979b). Other programs use a variety of chronological age cutoffs for administrative purposes. Even within the same agency, different services may define "aged" differently. These discrepancies often reflect societal age norms, which vary according to the system involved. In complex industrialized societies, plural age-grading systems usually develop relative to multiple social institutions (Newgarten and Hagestad, 1976). Thus, a person may be "old" at different chronological ages depending on the purposes of the particular system, such as education, economic, health, and family.

In spite of its shortcomings and inconsistencies, chronological age remains the basic legal and societal criterion for defining a person as old. In subsequent discussions in this book, unless otherwise specified, an older person is defined as one who is 65 or over.

History and Trends in Gerontology and Service Delivery Policy

Great interest in the processes of aging has been shown throughout history, but gerontology (the scientific study of aging and old people) did not develop as an academic area until the twentieth century. Earlier studies were largely grounded in philosophy and religion and centered on people whose length of life greatly exceeded the norm. Attempts to explain why some people lived much longer than most generated numerous myths and speculations concerning old age (Birren and Clayton, 1975). Historical trends in the development of gerontology are covered elsewhere; only a brief overview is presented in this work.[1] Table 1.1 summarizes some of the major developments in the field in the United States. During the late 1800s and early 1900s, studies of longevity, physiological changes with age, and differentiation between normal and pathological changes had been undertaken in England and Russia. By the 1920s, limited studies of physiological, social, and psychological aspects of aging were underway in the United States. During the 1920s and 1930s, two phenomena stimulated development of the field of gerontology. One involved increases in average life expectancy and a change in the leading causes of death, both of which were related to advances in the control of infectious diseases. The other phenomenon was the Great Depression, which directed attention to the economic and social needs of the growing number of older people.

In the early 1940s, conferences on aging were held by several scientific organizations, including the National Institutes of Health, the Medical Clinics of North America, and the American Orthopsychiatric Association. The growth of gerontology was slowed by World War II, although war-related studies contributed to greater understanding of the effects of aging and helped to lay the groundwork for postwar activities. In 1945, the Gerontological Society was founded, and in 1946, the National Institutes of Health established a Gerontological Research Unit (Birren and Clayton, 1975; Tibbitts, 1977a, b; Hendricks and Hendricks; 1977).

Recognition of gerontology as a field of academic study began in the 1940s in a few institutions of higher learning. In 1950, the government-sponsored National Conference on Aging focused attention on the emerging discipline of gerontology. In 1961, the first White House Conference on Aging produced a set of recommendations concerning development of a nationwide system of service delivery, education, and research for and about the aging (Tibbitts, 1977 a, b; White House Conference on Aging, 1973; U.S. DOL, 1976). Thus, the activities of the 1950s and early 1960s helped to clarify policy issues and to stimulate implementation of service programs for the aged. In addition, these activities documented the need for specialized training and education on aging and the aged.

[1]For a detailed history, see A. Achenbaum, *Shades of Gray: Old Age, American Values, and Federal Policies Since 1920* (Boston: Little, Brown and Co., 1982).

Table 1.1
Selected Developments in Gerontology in the United States

Prior to 1920
Scattered interest in vital statistics, biomedical factors, philosophy.

1920s
Increasing interest in medicine, psychology; shift in causes of death with control of infectious diseases.

1930s
Continuation of trends of 1920s. Influences of the New Deal felt. Interest developing in the social sciences. Several national conferences on aging research held.

1940s
Increasing interest by government and academic organizations. Public Health Service and National Institutes of Health (NIH) supported conferences and research. Professional association activity developed—interrupted by World War II, then revived in postwar period. In 1946, NIH started gerontological unit; Gerontological Society founded in 1945.

1950s
Between 1950 and 1960 production of literature on aging equaled that for preceding 115 years (Birren and Clayton, 1975).
1950 First National Conference on Aging held.
1951 Federal Committee on Aging established.
1952 First National Conference of State Commissions on Aging held.
1956 Federal Council on Aging replaced the 1951 Committee.
1956 Special Staff on Aging established within DHEW.
1958 Legislation called for White House Conference on Aging.
1959 Senate Special Committee on Aging established.

1960s
By 1960, every state had a unit on aging (some temporary) for White House Conference planning.
1961   First White House Conference on Aging recommended legislation establishing a national program of services for older persons.
1963   Kennedy gave message to Congress calling for legislation.
1963–64 Several bills presented in Congress but none passed.
1965   Landmark legislation: Older Americans Act passed.

1970s
1971 Second White House Conference on Aging held.
1973 Comprehensive amendments added to Older Americans Act.
1974 National Institute on Aging established.
1978 Major amendments added to Older Americans Act.

1980s
1981 Third White House Conference on Aging held.
1981 Additional amendments to Older Americans Act continued trends apparent in 1973 and 1978 amendments.

The Older Americans Act and Other Federal Legislation

The Older Americans Act of 1965 was a landmark in policy implementation. This act established the Administration on Aging and initiated what has become the federal-state-local "aging service delivery network." Table 1.2 summarizes the major provisions of the act as legislated in 1965 and as modified in subsequent amendments. Through the various sets of amendments, the Older Americans Act has retained its basic objectives with only minor revisions. These objectives, paraphrased, state that, consistent with our traditional concept of the inherent dignity of the individual, it is the responsibility of our nation to assist older persons by providing access to the following: (1) adequate retirement income, (2) physical and mental health services, (3) suitable housing, (4) restorative services, (5) employment opportunities, (6) retirement with honor and dignity, (7) meaningful activity in civic, cultural, and recreational areas, (8) efficient services including transportation, a choice of living arrangements, and coordinated social assistance, (9) immediate benefit from research findings, and (10) freedom in planning and managing their own lives (U.S. DHEW, 1979b).

In the early years of the Older Americans Act, many of its programs were largely exploratory. As experience was gained in service delivery, demonstration, research, and training, the legislation was modified. At the same time, various special-interest groups (such as service providers, senior advocacy groups, institutions of higher learning, and housing developers) lobbied to influence policies related to the act (Estes, 1979). A trend toward greater emphasis on planning and coordination became apparent when the 1969 amendments provided for "area-wide model projects." These were the forerunners of area agencies on aging, which were mandated in the 1973 amendments and which were to become principal components of the service delivery and resource allocation systems for the aging. Experience with congregate nutrition demonstration projects contributed documentation for the 1972 congregate meals title, later to become part of the 1973 amendments. Although the programs developed through the Older Americans Act have always emphasized services for the "most needy" older population, the legislation clearly states that services are intended for *all* older Americans and does not permit a test of means adequacy. Appropriation levels for the various Older Americans Act programs for fiscal years 1981, 1982, and 1983 are shown in Table 1.3.

In the mid 1970s, the focus on the most needy was sharpened, and an initially informal policy shift permitted greater Older Americans Act program involvement in health-related activities. This shift was formalized when the 1978 amendments placed high priority on the

Table 1.2
The Evolution of the Older Americans Act in Terms of Major
Provisions and Most Significant Amendments, 1965–1981

1965		1969		1973	
Title	Content	Title	Content	Title	Content
I	Objectives, definitions	I	Objectives, definitions	I	Objectives, definitions
II	Establishment of Administration on Aging (AoA) in DHEW and statement of AoA functions	II	More specific duties for AoA	II	Revision of duties and position of AoA to include items from previous Title VII; establishment of National Clearinghouse and Federal Council on the Aging
III	Community service grants to states	III	Revision of community services to require more specific state plans; addition of areawide model projects		
IV	Research and demonstration grants	IV	Research and demonstration grants	III	Revision of community services to call for Planning and Service Areas (PSA's), Area Agencies on Aging (AAA's), more local control, model projects (innovative service delivery added)
V	Career training grants	V	Slight change in training grants, decentralization		
VI	General provisions (Advisory Council, etc.)	VI	Addition of *new* volunteer programs, such as Retired Senior Volunteer Program (RSVP)	IV	Training and research grants: (a) training (b) research (c) multidisciplinary center programs
		VII	General provisions	V	Multipurpose centers

(*continued page 8*)

1978		1981	
Title	Content	Title	Content
I	Objectives, definitions	I	Objectives, definitions
II	Expansion of duties; addition of health and interagency agreements; emphasis on continuum of care	II	Minor changes in duties; elimination of National Clearinghouse; reduction of functions of Federal Council on Aging
III	Combination of previous Titles III, V, and VII; addition of home meals and requirement that 50 percent of special service funds be targeted for access, in-home, and legal services	III	Similar to 1978 Title III, with minor changes: elimination of 50 percent requirements; combination of home meals and congregate meals provisions; change from term "social services" to "supportive services"
IV	Training, research, and discretionary grants: (a) training (b) research and development (c) projects of national significance (d) mortgage insurance and interest subsidies for senior centers	IV	Training, research, and discretionary grants; continuation of trend toward increased emphasis on health-related areas and support services for frail elderly: (a) training (b) research, demonstration and other activities (comprehensive long-term-care projects, legal services demonstration projects, national impact projects, and utility and home heating cost demonstration projects) (c) appropriations and general provisions
V	Community Service Employment Program		
VI	Special grants for Indian social services		
		V	Community service employment program
		VI	Special grants for Indian social services

Table 1.2 (*continued*)

1965		1969		1973	
Title	Content	Title	Content	Title	Content
				VI	Volunteer programs
				VII	Nutrition programs
				VIII	Repeal of prior Title VII
				IX	Community Service Employment Program

Note: Relatively minor amendments made in 1967, 1975, and 1977 are not included here.

noninstitutional components of a continuum of care for the "vulnerable" elderly. General trends in the evolution of the Older Americans Act between 1965 and 1981 included more emphasis on planning and coordination at a decentralized level, concentration on the "vulnerable" elderly, and the development of a continuum of care, including health-related services and the maintenance of the older individual in the "least restrictive environment" (U.S. Congress, 1982; U.S. DHEW, 1979b; U.S. DHEW, 1980). Although the "aging network" developed through the Administration on Aging is the focal point for service programs, it is by no means the only source of services. A large number of federal categorical grant programs also have supported social services for the elderly. Estes identified 80 programs listed in the 1978 *Catalog of Federal Domestic Assistance* that directly or indirectly provided benefits for older persons (1979). Some of these were consolidated by the Omnibus Budget Reconciliation Act of 1981 (Public Law 97-35), which redirected 57 health, education, and social service programs into nine "block grants."

Block Grants. Block grants reduce the extent of federal regulation, permitting greater discretion in use of funds by state governments. Under the block grant program, federal funding is provided for a wide range of activities within a broadly defined purpose, states have considerable discretion in program design and resource allocation,

Table 1.3
Appropriation Levels for Older Americans Act Programs, Fiscal
Years 1981, 1982, and 1983 (in millions of dollars)

	FY 1981 appropriation	FY 1982 continuing resolution level	FY 1983 further continuing resolution level
Title II:			
National Clearinghouse	$ 1.8	$ 1.7	0
Federal Council on Aging	0.481	0.191	$ 0.175
Title III:			
State administration	22.7	21.673	21.673
Social services	251.5	240.869	240.869
Congregate meals	295.00	286.749	319.074
Home-delivered meals	55.0	57.350	62.025
Title IV: Training, research, and discretionary projects	40.5	22.175	22.175
Title V: Community services employment	277.1	277.1[a]	319.500
Title VI: Grants to Indian tribes	6.0	5.735	5.735

[a]Represents estimated annual expenditures by Title V program for fiscal year 1982. The actual amount in the continuing resolution is $66,500,000; Title V received funds under the fiscal year 1981 appropriation through June 30, 1982. The $66,500,000 available under the continuing resolution will fund the project from July 1 through Sept. 30, 1982.

Source: U.S. Senate, Special Committee on Aging, *The Proposed Fiscal Year 1983 Budget: What It Means for Older Americans* (Washington, D.C.: U.S. Government Printing Office, 1982) and U.S. Department of Health and Human Services, "Report on Activities in Aging: A Report to the House Committee on Appropriations" (Washington, D.C.: Administration on Aging, January, 1983, unpublished).

federal reporting and monitoring requirements are minimal, and federal agency administrative discretion is highly limited (U.S. DHHS, 1982a; Florida Advisory Council on Intergovernmental Relations, 1982).

Block grants may be used for services for eligible persons of all ages, but the following five block grant programs initiated in fiscal year 1982 have particular potential for substantial impact on services for the elderly.

1. *The Social Services Block Grant* provides for services to help people maintain self-sufficiency; to prevent neglect, abuse, or exploitation of children and adults who are unable to protect their own interests; and to prevent inappropriate institutionalization. This program revises the previous social services program under Title

XX of the Social Security Act, repealing previous Title XX regulations and combining the previously separate social service, training, and day-care provisions. Under the block grant, each state defines the services to be funded and the eligibility requirements.

2. *The Community Service Block Grant* provides for programs in the areas of nutrition, housing, and employment to improve the condition of low-income persons. This program replaced several programs previously funded under the Economic Opportunity Act of 1965.

3. *The Low Income Home Energy Assistance Block Grant* provides funds to help low-income people meet the costs of home energy. This program also replaced selected programs previously funded under the Economic Opportunity Act of 1965.

4. *The Alcohol and Drug Abuse and Mental Health Services Block Grant* provides for care of the mentally ill, for promotion of mental health, and for efforts to combat alcohol and drug abuse. This program incorporates programs previously funded under the Community Mental Health Centers Act, Sections 301 and 312 of the Comprehensive Alcohol Abuse and Alcoholism Prevention Treatment and Rehabilitation Act of 1970, and Sections 409 and 410 of the Drug Abuse, Prevention, Treatment, and Rehabilitation Act.

5. *The Preventive Health and Health Services Block Grant* provides for public health services to reduce preventable illness, disability, and death and to improve the quality of life. This program replaces eight federal health programs including emergency medical services, hypertension control, rodent control, and home health services (Florida Advisory Council on Intergovernmental Relations, 1982; Florida Department of Health and Rehabilitative Services, 1982; U.S. DHHS, 1982a).

In addition to federally funded programs, local government agencies, private service organizations, and religious organizations are involved in service delivery, and increasing recognition is being given to the "informal" services provided by family, friends, and neighbors. Table 1.4 summarizes the sources of services reported by older persons in the oft-quoted "Cleveland Study" carried out by the U.S. General Accounting Office. The General Accounting Office concluded that "home help types of services and transportation were provided by the family or friends. Medical and social/recreational services were provided mostly by agencies. Financial assistance and assessment and referral services were split about evenly between family and friends and an agency" (1977c: 18).

Table 1.4
Services Received by Type of Service and Source: Older Persons in
Cleveland, Ohio, 1975 (percent of respondents, $N = 1609$)

	Family/friends	Agency	Both	Total
Medical services				
Medical care	——	75	——	75
Psychotropic drugs	——	20	——	20
Supportive devices	——	15	——	15
Nursing care	3	3	1	7
Physical therapy	——	4	——	4
Mental health	——	3	——	3
Home-help services				
Personal care	56	1	1	58
Checking	44	1	1	46
Homemaker	20	5	1	26
Administrative and legal	15	7	1	23
Meal preparation	13	8	1	22
Continuous supervision	6	1	1	8
Financial assistance				
General financial	2	7	——	9
Housing	12	10	——	22
Groceries and food stamps	7	8	——	15
Assessment and referral				
Coordination, information, and referral	8	3	1	12
Overall evaluation	——	8	——	8
Outreach	——	5	——	5
Social/recreational (formal organized activities outside the home)	——	30	——	30
Transportation	60	3	5	68

Source: U.S. General Accounting Office, *The Well-Being of Older People in Cleveland, Ohio* (Washington, D.C.: U.S. Government Printing Office, 1977).

Demographic Factors

The position of the aged in society has been influenced by the interaction of demographic factors with basic societal structures. Developments in the economic, political, educational, and family systems all affect and are affected by changes in the population's age structure. A combination of declining birth rates and lower death rates has resulted in substantial increases in the number and proportion of older persons in the United States during the twentieth century. The control of infectious diseases resulted in reductions in infant, childhood, and young-adult mortality, so that many more people could "survive" to old age. Average life expectancy from birth increased from about 47 in 1900 to 68 in 1950 and to about 74 in 1979 (U.S. DHHS, 1980c). Table 1.5 illustrates that much of the increase was related to reduction of deaths in early life. That is, people who would have died in infancy or early life in an earlier historical

Table 1.5
Expectation of Life at Selected Ages by Color and Sex: Death Registration in States, 1900–1902, and in United States, 1959–1961, 1969–1971, and 1978

Life table values and age	Total	White		All other	
		Male	Female	Male	Female
At birth					
1978	73.30	70.20	77.80	65.00	73.60
1969–1971	70.75	67.94	75.49	60.98	69.05
1959–1961	69.89	67.55	74.19	61.48	66.47
1900–1902[a]	49.24	48.23	51.08	32.54	32.54
At age 1 year					
1978	73.30	70.10	77.60	65.50	74.00
1969–1971	71.19	68.33	75.66	62.13	70.01
1959–1961	70.75	68.34	74.68	63.50	68.10
1900–1902[a]	55.20	54.61	56.39	42.46	43.54
At age 20 years					
1978	55.00	52.00	59.10	47.40	55.60
1969–1971	53.00	50.22	57.24	44.37	51.85
1959–1961	52.58	50.25	56.29	45.78	50.07
1900–1902[a]	42.79	42.19	43.77	34.11	36.89
At age 65 years					
1978	16.30	14.00	18.40	14.10	18.00
1969–1971	15.00	13.02	16.93	12.87	15.99
1959–1961	14.39	12.97	15.88	12.84	15.12
1900–1902[a]	11.86	11.51	12.23	10.38	11.38

[a]The 1900–1902 figures for "all other male" and "all other female" include only the black population, which comprised 95 percent or more of the "nonwhite" population.
Source: U.S. Department of Health and Human Services, National Center for Health Statistics, "Life Tables," *Vital Statistics of the United States, 1978*, Vol. II, Sec. 5, DHHS Pub. No. (PHS) 81-1104 (Hyattsville, MD: NCHS, 1980).

period were now surviving to old age, but once they reached age 65, these people had no striking increases in expected years remaining. From 1900 to 1960, the average expectation of life from birth increased by 25 years, but the average expectation of life remaining beyond age 65 increased by just 2½ years. Only recently have advances in health care, changes in lifestyle, and general improvement of social and economic conditions contributed to extension of life expectancy beyond age 65. Tables 1.6 and 1.7 reflect demographic trends in the growth of the number of older persons and, in particular, of the very-old population.

In terms of absolute numbers, the population age 65 and over increased from just over 3.0 million in 1900 to 25.5 million in 1980. It is predicted that the number will reach nearly 32.5 million by 2000 and 55.8 million in the year 2030. The fastest growing population segment is the group age 85 and above, with a projected increase of 84 percent between 1977 and 2000. This compares with a projected 28 percent increase for all persons age 60 and above (see Table 1.6). The *proportion* of older persons to the total population depends on relationships among death rates, birth rates, and migration. Between 1900 and 1980, the percent of the United States population age 65 and over nearly tripled, increasing from 4.1 percent to 11.3 percent. If current trends continue, at least 18 percent of the nation's population will be 65 or over by 2030 (U.S. DHHS, 1982b). In 1980, the number of older Americans (using the Adminstration on Aging definition of age 60 and above rather than the age 65 and above definition) was for the first time in history greater than the number of children age 10 and under and the number of persons age 11 to 19. Each of these three age groups (60 plus, 0 to 10, and 11 to 19) numbered around 35 million persons in 1980, but the oldest group was increasing more rapidly than the other two (U.S. DHHS, 1981).

In addition to the aging of the general population, two other demographic processes have special significance for social services. These are the differences in life expectancy by sex and the rapid growth of aged minority populations. In 1980, there were 148 females age 65 and above for every 100 males in that age category in the United States. By the year 2000, this ratio is expected to exceed 150 per 100. Compared with their male counterparts, older females are much more likely to live alone or with nonrelatives and to be widowed (U.S. DHHS, 1982b). The Administration on Aging reports that "clearly, future growth in the number of elderly women will increase the number of elderly who will require a variety of supportive services in order to cope with such difficulties as living alone in declining health and with low incomes" (U.S. DHEW, 1978: 7).

Whereas information for some specific minorities is scarce, data on the black population in general are readily available and at least

Table 1.6
The Older Population of the United States by Age Category, 1900–1977, with Projections to 2035: Number and
Percent of Total U.S. Population

	Age 60 +		Age 65 +		Age 75 +		Age 85 +	
	Number	Percent	Number	Percent	Number	Percent	Number	Percent
1900	4,879,000	6.4	3,084,000	4.0	895,000	1.2	122,000	0.2
1977	32,793,000	15.1	23,431,000	10.8	8,853,000	4.1	2,040,000	0.9
2000	41,973,000	16.1	31,822,000	12.2	14,386,000	5.5	3,756,000	1.4
2035	70,514,000	23.2	55,805,000	18.3	26,178,000	8.6	6,854,000	2.3

Source: U.S. Department of Health, Education and Welfare, Administration on Aging, "Some Prospects for the Future Elderly Population," in *Statistical Reports on Older Americans,* No. 3, DHEW Pub. No. (OHDS) 78-20288 (Washington, D.C.: U.S. Government Printing Office, 1978).

Table 1.7

Percent Increase in the Size of the Older Population of the United States for Selected Periods, with Projections to 2035

	Age 60 +	Age 65 +	Age 75 +	Age 85 +
1900–1977	572.1	659.8	889.2	1572.1
1977–2000	28.0	35.8	62.5	84.1
2000–2035	68.0	75.4	82.0	82.5
1977–2035	115.0	138.2	195.7	236.0

Source: U.S. Department of Health, Education and Welfare, Administration on Aging, "Some Prospects for the Future Elderly Population," in Statistical Reports on Older Americans, No. 3, DHEW Pub. No (OHDS) 78-20288 (Washington, D.C.: U.S. Government Printing Office, 1978).

reasonably accurate. Average life expectancy from birth for blacks increased from about 53 years in 1940 to 61 years in 1950, 64 years in 1960, 65 years in 1970, and 69 years in 1978. Between 1940 and 1978, the difference between whites and blacks in expectation of life from birth declined from approximately 10 years to about 4 years. The growth rate of the nonwhite older population is much more rapid than that of the white older population, with a projected increase of about 64 percent between 1977 and 2000 (U.S. DHEW, 1978). Improved living standards and health care have contributed to increasing survival of other minority groups as well. Thus, service program personnel must consider the cultural and value orientations of groups such as blacks, Hispanic Americans, American Indians, Asian Americans, and others in developing and delivering services for older people.[2]

Rationale and Organization of This Book

Although the literature on gerontology and aging has grown rapidly, much of this literature does not address the practical issues faced by service delivery personnel, nor does it relate these issues to more abstract conceptual and policy considerations. This text is intended to help fill these gaps, using a frame of reference that may be called "social-gerontological" in that it draws on concepts from

[2]For a detailed discussion of ethnic considerations, see Donald Gelfand, Aging: The Ethnic Factor (Boston: Little, Brown and Co., 1982).

multiple disciplines and professions, including sociology, social work, political science, psychology, demography, public health, planning, and public administration.

This introductory chapter documents the growth of the older population and general societal responses to the needs of the aged. Chapters 2 and 3 set the stage for subsequent discussion by examining current concepts in service delivery, planning, and evaluation. Chapters 4 through 9 provide overviews of the major categories of social services to be found in most communities, along with discussions of needs, goals, and resources relative to the various service areas. Chapter 10, by Wilma Donahue, reminds the reader of the need to respect the rights and dignity of service recipients. The final chapter presents a broad descriptive summary of occupations in the study of aging and in delivery of services to older people.

References

Atchley, Robert C. *The Social Forces in Later Life*, 3rd ed. Belmont, CA: Wadsworth Publishing Co., 1980.

Binstock, R. H., and E. Shanas, eds. *Handbook of Aging and the Social Sciences*. New York: Van Nostrand Reinhold Co., 1976.

Birren, J., and V. Clayton. "History of Gerontology." In *Aging: Scientific Perspectives and Social Issues*, eds. D. S. Woodruff and J. E. Birren, pp. 15–27. New York: D. Van Nostrand Co., 1975.

Estes, C. L. *The Aging Enterprise*. San Francisco: Jossey-Bass Publishers, 1979.

Florida Advisory Council on Intergovernmental Relations. *Florida's Implementation of the Federal Block Grants*. Tallahassee, FL: State of Florida, 1982.

Florida Department of Health and Rehabilitative Services. *Social Services (Title XX) Block Grant Pre-Expenditure Report, July 1, 1982 to June 30, 1983*. Tallahassee, FL: State of Florida, 1982.

Hendricks, J., and C. D. Hendricks. *Aging in Mass Society*. Cambridge, MA: Winthrop Publishers, 1977.

––––––. *Aging in Mass Society*, 2nd ed. Cambridge, MA: Winthrop Publishers, 1981.

Maddox, G., and J. Wiley. "Scope, Concepts and Methods in the Study of Aging." In *Handbook of Aging and the Social Sciences*, eds. R. H. Binstock and E. Shanas, pp. 3–34. New York: Van Nostrand Reinhold Co., 1976.

Newgarten, B. L., and G. O. Hagestad. "Age and the Life Course." In *Handbook of Aging and the Social Sciences*, eds. R. H. Binstock and E. Shanas, pp. 35–55. New York: Van Nostrand Reinhold Co., 1976.

Schultz, J. H. *The Economics of Aging*, 2nd ed. Belmont, CA: Wadsworth Publishing Co., 1980.

Tibbitts, C., ed. *Handbook of Social Gerontology: Societal Aspects of Aging.* Chicago: The University of Chicago Press, 1960.

_____. "Aging in America: Present and Future." Address delivered at California State University, Chico, CA, November 11, 1977a.

_____. "Introduction." In *Ethical Consideration in Long Term Care*, eds. W. E. Winston and A. J. E. Wilson III, pp. 1–16. St. Petersburg, FL: Eckerd College Gerontology Center, 1977b.

U.S. Congress, Committee on Education and Labor. *Compilation of the Older Americans Act of 1965 and Related Provisions of Law as Amended through December 29, 1981.* Washington, D.C.: U.S. Government Printing Office, 1982.

U.S. Department of Health and Human Services, Adminstration on Aging. *Facts about Older Americans, 1979*, DHHS Pub. No. (PHS) 80-20006. Washington, D.C.: U.S. Government Printing Office, 1980a.

_____. National Center for Health Statistics. "Life Tables." In *Vital Statistics of the United States, 1978*, Vol. II, Sec. 5, DHHS Pub. No. (PHS) 81-1104. Hyattsville, MD: NCHS, 1980b.

_____. National Center for Health Statistics. *Monthly Vital Statistics Report, Provisional Statistics: Annual Summary for the United States, 1979*, DHHS Pub. No. (PHS) 81-1120. Hyattsville, MD: NCHS, November 13, 1980c.

_____. Office of Human Development Services, Administration on Aging. "Older Americans Month May, 1981, Information Package."Washington, D.C.: AoA, 1981.

_____. "Block Grants Programs; Final Rules." *Federal Register*, Vol. 47, No. 129, July 6, 1982a, pp. 29472–29493.

_____. Administration on Aging. "Facts about Older Americans, 1980–81." Washington, D.C.: AoA, 1982b (draft).

U.S. Department of Health, Education and Welfare, Administration on Aging. "Some Prospects for the Future Elderly Population." In *Statistical Reports on Older Americans*, No. 3, DHEW Pub. No. (OHDS) 78-20288. Washington, D.C.: U.S. Government Printing Office, 1978.

_____. Administration on Aging. *Inventory of Federal Statistical Programs Relating to Older Persons.* Washington, D.C.: U.S. Government Printing Office, 1979a.

_____. Administration on Aging. *Older Americans Act of 1965, as Amended: History and Related Acts*, DHEW Pub. No. (OHDS) 79-20170. Washington, D.C.: U.S. Government Printing Office, 1979b.

_____. Office of Human Development Services. "Grants for State and Community Programs on Aging: Rules and Regulations." *Federal Register*, Vol. 45, No. 63, March 31, 1980, pp. 21126–21166.

U.S. Department of Labor. *Occupational Outlook Quarterly Special Issue: Working with Older People.* Washington, D.C.: U.S. Government Printing Office, Fall, 1976.

U.S. General Accounting Office. *Conditions of Older People: National Information System Needed.* Washington, D.C.: U.S. Government Printing Office, 1977a.

_____. *Home Health—The Need for a National Policy to Better Provide for the Elderly.* Washington, D.C.: U.S. Government Printing Office, 1977b.

_____. *The Well-Being of Older People in Cleveland, Ohio.* Washington, D.C.: U.S. Government Printing Office, 1977c.

U.S. Senate, Special Committee on Aging. *The Proposed Fiscal Year 1983 Budget: What It Means for Older Americans.* Washington, D.C.: U.S. Government Printing Office, 1982.

White House Conference on Aging. *Toward a National Policy on Aging. Proceedings of the 1971 White House Conference on Aging*, Vol. II. Washington, D.C.: U.S. Government Printing Office, 1973.

Chapter

2

The Service Delivery Setting and Related Concepts

Services may be delivered to older people in a variety of settings, and the majority are served in more than one setting. For example, a person may participate in congregate-meal, educational, and recreational programs at a senior center; receive health education and preventive health services at a neighborhood health center; and receive home-chore or home-repair services in his or her home. The nomenclature that has developed in the aging service delivery network often mixes bases for classification, thus complicating and confusing the process of service monitoring and evaluation. For example, the rules and regulations for social services under the Older Americans Act (1978 amendments) provide for in-home services, senior center services, legal services, and nutrition services (U.S. DHEW, 1980). A full range of services, including nutrition and legal services, may be delivered in the home and in the senior center service delivery setting. Obviously, the intent of the Administration on Aging in using these categories was to ensure that services would be provided both in senior centers and in the homes of older people. Certain functions are by definition home delivered, such as visiting-homemaker or home-chore services. The use of the terms "in-home" and "senior center" is potentially confusing because the reporting system includes services that may be delivered in either setting.

In general, services should be provided in the setting that is the most efficient and yet maintains the maximum independence and convenience for the client. The setting that meets these criteria may be an institution, a senior center, a clinic or office, a rehabilitation center, an adult day care center, or a private household. One state's response to the requirements of the Older Americans Act is illus-

Table 2.1
Structure of Service Delivery under the Older Americans Act, Title III-B and -C, State of Florida, Fiscal Years 1981–1983

Service	Client's home (independent residence)	Congregate facility (group home or institution)	Community group (senior center, other)
	Service delivery setting		
Access	X	X	X
Counseling	X	X	X
Chores	X		
Congregate meals		X	X
Day care			X
Education		X	X
Employment			X
Health support	X	X	X
Home-delivered meals	X		
Home health aide	X		
Homemaker	X		
Legal services	X	X	X
Nutrition education		X	X
Recreation		X	X
Shopping assistance			X
Telephone reassurance	X		
Visiting	X	X	

Source: Adapted from Florida Department of Health and Rehabilitative Services, *State Plan on Aging under Title III of the Older Americans Act for Florida, Fiscal Years 1981–83* (Tallahassee, FL: State of Florida, June, 1980).

trated in Table 2.1. In this example, legal services, counseling, and health support services under Title III-B of the Act are listed as being provided in the home, in the community, and in "care providing facilities." Access services encompass all service delivery settings (Florida Department of Health and Rehabilitative Services, 1980).

The Continuum of Services

The concept of a continuum of services and care is broader than that of a "comprehensive and coordinated service delivery system," which is illustrated in Table 2.1. This concept is not restricted to programs under the state Older Americans Act plan. With a continuum, any given community should have available a full range of preventive, supportive, and restorative services. In actuality, the array of services contained in the continuum forms multiple continua rather than a single continuum. Terms such as community support system and constellation of services might be more appropriate, since they imply that a range of services is available to meet widely varied situations (Tibbitts, 1977a).

The array of services included in the continuum is familiar to most service delivery personnel (Friedsam, 1977). The following list groups the components according to the frame of reference used in this book.

A. Access services
    1. Information and referral
    2. Outreach
    3. Case coordination and service management
    4. Transportation
    5. Escort
B. Health services
    1. Hospital services
    2. Nursing home services
    3. Physician services
    4. Rehabilitation therapists' services
    5. Health education services
    6. Home health services
C. Nutrition services
    1. Congregate meals
    2. Home-delivered meals
    3. Nutrition education
D. Housing services
    1. Independent residential facilities
    2. Assisted residential facilities
    3. Personal care homes
    4. Home repair services
    5. Adult day care
E. Income maintenance services
    1. Pensions
    2. Old Age and Survivors Insurance (Social Security)
    3. Supplementary Security Income
    4. Indirect income
        a. Rental and mortgage assistance programs
        b. Discounts
        c. Tax reductions

F. Employment services
  1. Community service employment programs
  2. CETA
  3. U.S. Employment Service Older Worker Program
  4. Job banks, etc.
G. Personal support services
  1. Counseling
  2. Peer support
  3. Telephone reassurance
  4. Friendly visiting
  5. Personal advocacy
H. Training and education
  1. Training for employment
  2. Training for self-care
  3. Adult education

Obviously, the categories overlap. For example, nutrition education is both a nutrition service and an educational service; community service employment is both an employment service and an income maintenance service; nursing homes provide both housing and health care. Later in this book, an overview of program goals, structures, and legislation is presented for each of the major categories.

Service Coordination

Coordination of services is intended to ensure that older persons differing widely in functional capacity, environment, and availability of informal supports receive an integrated package of services appropriate to their unique situations. The proportion of elderly needing assistance in activities of daily living (ADL) is given in Figure 2.1. In order to meet the goals of service coordination, some agency must carry out service management (also called case management) functions. A service manager is responsible for assessing a client's physical, social, and psychological status; for developing a plan for services to be delivered; and for evaluating the acceptability and effectiveness of the package for the client. In developing the plan, the service manager attempts to enhance the client's capacity for independence and self-care and to integrate informal services from family, neighbors, and church groups with the services of the formal system. The resulting plan may combine services delivered by multiple agencies in multiple settings. For example, a client with a substantial degree of impairment may be taken to a senior center for educational, recreational, and socialization services and may have a midday meal at

Figure 2.1   Percent of Elderly Needing Assistance in Four Activities of Daily Living by Age Groups: United States, 1978

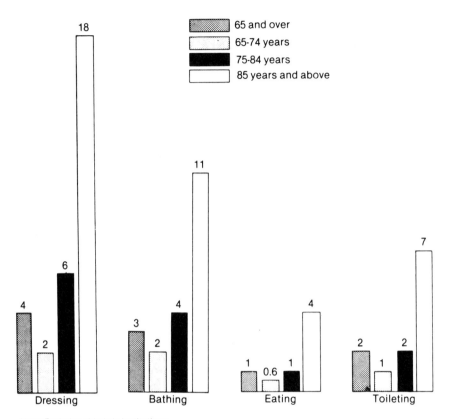

Note: Excludes elderly in institutions.

Source: U.S. Department of Health and Human Services, Federal Council on Aging, *The Need for Long Term Care* (Washington, D.C.: U.S. Government Printing Office, 1981), p. 31.

the center. That client may also receive "meals on wheels" for the evening meal, home-chore services, and home-delivered personal care services (such as assistance in bathing and dressing). If relatives or neighbors are available and willing, they may help to provide transportation, home chores, or personal care. In all cases, the goal of service management and the continuum-of-care concept is to maintain the older person at an optimal level of independence in the least restrictive environment possible (Philadelphia Geriatric Center, 1978; U.S. DHEW, 1980).

Alternatives to Institutional Care

The term "alternatives to institutional care" became popular in the 1970s; some assumed that the alternatives of home and community care could entirely replace institutional care.[1] It has since been suggested that this assumption was unfounded and that the institution is and will remain an important part of the continuum of services. The objective in developing community-based and home-delivered services is to avoid inappropriate use of institutions and to provide persons needing assistance with a choice of service settings (Wilson, 1971; Friedsam, 1977). In the past and in many places at present, the lack of coordinated support services in the community has meant that a person who could get by at home with a little help had to be institutionalized because that help was either not available or not accessible (Kent, 1971; Hammerman, 1974; U.S. Senate, 1976a; Wilson, 1977).

Tibbitts commented on the alternatives concept as follows:

> The phrase "alternatives to institutional care" probably gained currency when family and institutional care were about the only methods of providing for chronically and severely impaired older persons. Are we reaching a point at which we can focus on community services for impaired older persons living in their own homes or with their own families as the primary mode of meeting their needs and reverse the phrase by regarding institutions as "alternatives to community care" utilized only when they can be justified by patient need? (Tibbitts, 1977b: 14)

Institutional care is intended for persons who have severe impairment of functioning and are incapable of managing their own activities of daily living. The purpose of the institution is to provide comprehensive personal and health care for the most dependent segment of the older population. The types of services provided in institutions could be provided in other settings including patients' homes, but the costs, logistics, and availability of skilled caretakers generally preclude this arrangement. The widely quoted U.S. General Accounting Office study, as shown in Figure 2.2, predicts the cost factor quite well. The straight line (level) for costs of institutional

---

[1]For a more detailed discussion of this topic, see T. Koff, *Long Term Care* (Boston, MA: Little, Brown and Co., 1982).

Figure 2.2   Comparison of Estimated Monthly Cost of Home Services and Institutionalization at Each Impairment Level per Individual

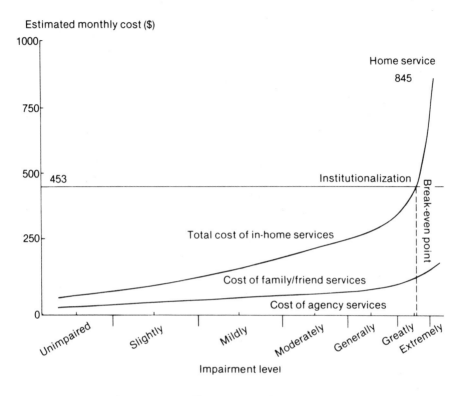

Source: U.S. General Accounting Office, *Home Health—The Need for a National Policy to Better Provide for the Elderly* (Washington, D.C.: U.S. Government Printing Office, 1977), p. 18.

care, however, may be subject to question, since more severely impaired persons often require extra-cost institutional services. For persons with relatively low or moderate levels of functional impairment, home/community care costs less than institutional care. For those with severe levels of impairment, the cost of home care increases dramatically; for the most severely impaired, it far exceeds the cost of institutional care (1977).

Long-term care institutions include chronic disease hospitals, nursing homes, and homes for the aged. Personal care homes have some of the characteristics of institutions but are less restrictive and promote maintenance of independence to whatever extent is possible.

Deinstitutionalization

The deinstitutionalization movement applies to a variety of institutions, although currently it is directed toward mental hospitals. At one time, substantial numbers of people experienced prolonged confinement in tuberculosis hospitals. Drugs introduced in the 1950s made it possible to bring pulmonary tuberculosis under control on a largely outpatient basis, and the huge tuberculosis hospital essentially disappeared. Psychotropic drugs were expected to have a parallel effect on mental hospitals in the 1960s for the treatment of the major functional psychoses. These medications did help to reduce both the number of mental hospital patients and the average length of hospitalization. The psychiatric drugs, however, were applied mainly to functional disorders more prevalent among younger persons, and public mental hospitals continued to house large numbers of older persons until the recent deinstitutionalization movement resulted in mass discharge of elderly patients. Some of these older patients had been admitted with functional mental disorders when they were young and had grown old in the institutions. Others were admitted during their advanced years with catch-all diagnoses of "senility" or organic brain syndrome. The fact that these hospitalized people often received little or no treatment and only minimal custodial care provided the rationale for deinstitutionalization (Donahue, 1977, 1978; Tibbitts, 1977a, b; Butler and Lewis, 1977; U.S. Senate, 1976b).

The deinstitutionalization movement of the 1970s has been viewed as a failure in policy implementation. A crisis was created by the movement because community service systems were unable to provide needed care (Donahue, 1978, 1979; Pepper, 1977; U.S. Senate, 1976b; Cohen, 1978). One critic of the movement, Herbert Shore, says, "The cult of alternatives to institutionalization polarized the system, raised false issues as to cost effectiveness and impeded the natural evolution of the institution into a true therapeutic environment" (Shore, 1981: 18). Donahue (1979) identifies incomplete planning, temptation of financial gain by the states through shifting costs of care from state to federal sources, pressures from special interests (for profit facilities), failure of community mental health centers, and community attitudes as contributing to the crisis.

Large numbers of older patients released from state mental hospitals were placed in nursing homes, leading some critics to refer to the movement as "deinstitutionalization by reinstitutionalization." Others wound up in poorly supervised, profit-making boarding homes either immediately upon discharge from the hospital or after a stay in a community nursing home (Pepper, 1977; Oriol, 1976). The future of the movement is still uncertain. Increasing attention has been given to improving services and treatment in hospitals and nursing homes as well as to increasing regulation and supervision of boarding homes and community services. The continuum-of-services concept has attempted to improve support services for vulnerable older persons in all settings but has emphasized community care.

Senior Centers

The multipurpose senior center emphasizes the provision at a particular location of many types of services, coordinated by a center director and staff. The center is sometimes characterized as a community or neighborhood focal point. Senior centers are often the sponsors of and the "headquarters" for home-delivered services as well. The basic package provided by multipurpose centers includes recreation, education, nutrition, preventive health services (screening, education, exercise), counseling, information and referral, and outreach services. Some centers incorporate adult day care and rehabilitation therapies as supplements to the basic package (U.S. DHEW, 1979; Crawford, 1976).

Summary

Most human services may be delivered in a variety of settings ranging from the patient's home to the hospital. Provided adequate finances, personnel, and facilities are available and accessible, it is preferable to enable the service recipient to maintain the "least restrictive environment." The needs and the environments vary according to the individual's resources, such as adaptive skills, informal supports, and community structure. In order to permit older persons to live in the least restrictive environment, it is essential for communities to have a full range of services and to have resources coordinated and accessed by a service management type of system. It is important to recognize that the range of services (often called the continuum of care) includes institutional care, which may be essential or preferred for a small proportion of the elderly. Mental hospitals and nursing homes in general have a poor reputation in the United States, and the deinstitutionalization movement of the 1970s attempted to move virtually all residents out of such facilities and into community settings with services referred to as "alternatives" to institutional care. Unfortunately, the movement was implemented with incomplete planning and was influenced by special interest groups that took advantage of opportunities for exploitation, financial gain, and self-promotion. Donahue refers to the "victims" of the movement as our "abandoned elderly," Cohen states that the policy makers created a monster, and Shore says that the movement sidetracked the development of institutions into a "true therapeutic environment" (Donahue, 1978; Cohen, 1978; Shore, 1981).

On the other hand, the so-called alternatives are meeting the needs of a substantial number of people who may have been unnecessarily confined to institutions. The system is evolving slowly and at times has used a trial-and-error approach. Indications are that a combination of institutional care, formal community-based services and supports, and increased use of informal service providers (family, neighbors, peers) will result in a human services system that is capable of providing options for the older person and maintenance of the least restrictive environment for each individual.

References

Butler, R. N. *Thoughts on Geriatric Medicine.* Washington, D.C.: National Institute on Aging, 1978.

Butler, R. N., and M. I. Lewis. *Aging and Mental Health*, 2nd ed. St. Louis: C. V. Mosby Co., 1977.

Cohen, E. S. "Teratogenesis and the Policy Makers" (editorial). *The Gerontologist* 18 (1978): 101, 120.

Crawford, C. O. "Creating and Maintaining Independent Living for Older Persons." In *Total Health and Aging*, eds. W. C. Martin and A. J. E. Wilson III, pp. 95–104. St. Petersburg, FL: Eckerd College Gerontology Center, 1976.

Donahue, W. T. "What about Our Responsibility Toward the Abandoned Elderly?" *The Gerontologist* 18 (1978): 102–111.

Donahue, W. T. "Deinstitutionalization—20th Century Mental Health Revolution." Paper presented at Baylor University, Waco, Texas, October 11, 1979.

Florida Department of Health and Rehabilitative Services. *State Plan on Aging under Title III of the Older Americans Act for Florida, Fiscal Years 1981–83.* Tallahassee, FL: State of Florida, June, 1980.

Friedsam, H. J. "Overview." In *Ethical Consideration in Long Term Care*, eds. W. E. Winston and A. J. E. Wilson III, pp. 185–192. St. Petersburg, FL: Eckerd College Gerontology Center, 1977.

Hammerman, J. "The Role of the Institution and the Concept of Parallel Services." *The Gerontologist* 14 (1974): 11–14.

Kaplan, J. "Alternatives to Nursing Home Care: Fact or Fiction" (editorial). *The Gerontologist* 12 (1972): 114.

Kent, D. P. "Social and Family Concepts of Health Problems of the Aged." In *Health and the Family*, ed. C. O. Crawford, pp. 161–174. New York: Macmillan Co., 1971.

Kisten, H., and R. Morris. "Alternatives to Institutional Care for the Elderly and Disabled." *The Gerontologist* 12, Part I (1972): 139–142.

Oriol, W. E. "Total Health and Aging." In *Aging and Total Health*, eds. W. C. Martin and A. J. E. Wilson III, pp. 15–25. St. Petersburg, FL: Eckerd College Gerontology Center, 1976.

Pepper, C. "Legislation Needed to Correct a National Crisis in Adult Care Homes." *Congressional Record*, September 8, 1977, HG 05-1-52.

Shore, H. H. "Institutional Care: Folding Up or Forging Ahead?" *Generations: The Journal of the Western Gerontological Society* 5 (1981): 18–20, 43.

Tibbitts, C. "Aging in America: Present and Future." Address delivered at California State University, Chico, CA, November 11, 1977a.

_____. "Introduction." In *Ethical Considerations in Long Term Care*, eds. W. E. Winston and A. J. E. Wilson III, pp. 1–16. St. Petersburg, FL: Eckerd College Gerontology Center, 1977b.

U.S. Department of Health and Human Services, Administration on Aging. "Information Memorandum on Long Term Care Policy." Washington, D.C.: AoA, November 25, 1980.

U.S. Department of Health, Education and Welfare, Administration on Aging. *Older Americans Act of 1965, as Amended: History and Related Acts*, DHEW Pub. No. (OHDS) 79-20170. Washington, D.C.: U.S. Government Printing Office, 1979.

_____, Office of Human Development Services. "Grants for State and Community Programs on Aging: Rules and Regulations." *Federal Register*, Vol. 45, No. 63, March 31, 1980, pp. 21126–21166.

U.S. General Accounting Office. *Home Health—The Need for a National Policy to Better Provide for the Elderly*. Washington, D.C.: U.S. Government Printing Office, 1977.

U.S. Senate, Special Committee on Aging. *Nursing Home Care in the United States: Failure in Public Policy*. Washington, D.C.: U.S. Government Printing Office, 1974.

_____, Special Committee on Aging. *Congregate Housing for Older Adults: Assisted Residential Living Combining Shelter and Services*. Washington, D.C.: U.S. Government Printing Office, 1975.

_____, Special Committee on Aging. *Adult Day Facilities for Treatment, Health Care, and Related Services*. Washington, D.C.: U.S. Government Printing Office, 1976a.

_____, Special Committee on Aging. "The Role of Nursing Homes in Caring for Discharged Mental Patients (and the Birth of a For-Profit Boarding Home Industry)." In *Nursing Home Care in the United States: Failure in Public Policy*, Supportive Paper No. 7. Washington, D.C.: U.S. Government Printing Office, 1976b.

Wilson, A. J. E., III. "Effects of Health Problems on the Family Life of Older People." In *Health and the Family*, ed. C. O. Crawford, pp. 203–215. New York: Macmillan Co., 1971.

Chapter

3

Program Planning and Evaluation

Beattie describes social service planning for older persons as being primarily concerned with tapping financial, personal, and facility resources in order to assist the elderly in functioning at optimal levels. Planning should also provide opportunities for older people to continue to grow personally, to participate socially, and to contribute to society (Beattie, 1976).

Implicit in this definition is the idea that certain conditions or situations are present that interfere with or prevent older persons from optimal functioning and restrict their opportunities for meaningful activity and personal growth. Some of these conditions are loss of the work role, reduced income, ageism, social isolation, physical and mental impairments, and inadequate or nonexistent opportunities for involvement in the social system. The nature and extent of these conditions vary from community to community and from one type of older person to another. The term "older persons" brings together a group of great diversity in age itself as well as in social, cultural, educational, health, occupational, economic, racial, and ethnic characteristics.

Morris and Binstock (1966) suggest that the planning process involves six steps, or types of activity. These are problem identification, problem analysis, involvement of interested people, development of a plan for action, program implementation, and program evaluation. The activities called for by the Administration on Aging (AoA) in the state and area planning process under the Older Americans Act are similar to these, although the terminology is different. AoA regulations call for needs assessment, resource assessment, priority and objective setting, preparation of a plan with action steps, review of the plan by appropriate agencies and by the public, and provisions for monitoring and evaluation (U.S. DHEW, 1980b). The activities involved in the planning process do not necessarily occur in a fixed sequence, even though certain actions must be underway or completed before others can begin. In practice, the steps may overlap; in fact, schedules for planning usually include a time overlap. For example, needs assessments and resource assessments may be carried out simultaneously, whereas evaluation is a continuing operation overlapping all stages. The planning process may appear to be clearcut and relatively simple, but this is seldom true in practice. For a variety of reasons, many community service plans fail to include adequate or effective attention to at least some of the steps. This may occur because of inadequate funding for planning, lack of properly trained staff, time restraints in the planning-budgeting-implementing-evaluating cycle, influence of special interests, and rapid demographic and social change (Estes, 1973, 1974, 1979; Morris and Rein, 1968; Johnson, 1977). Morris and Rein also note that planning structures exist in a complex variety of organizations, with irrationalities, contradictions, and duplication often providing the basis for action (1968). They suggest that in most communities, multiple planning approaches and organizations (each associated with a special interest) compete for scarce funds.

The specific information needs of planning agencies vary according to the extent of the agency's responsibility, authority, and sponsorship. In this chapter, a broad comprehensive approach is taken, using the planning model of the Administration on Aging for area agencies on aging (AAA's). AAA's exist in all parts of the country except a few states in which a state unit carries out the AAA function for the entire state. Older Americans Act rules and regulations require that each state be divided into planning and service areas (PSA's) and that an area agency on aging be designated for each PSA. Under certain conditions, states may apply to the Administration on Aging for designation of the entire state as a single PSA, but only a few states have done this. The AAA's are charged with "developing and administering the area plan for a comprehensive and coordinated system of services" and for serving as "the advocate and focal point for older persons in the planning and service area" (U.S. DHEW, 1980b: 21154). The legislative charge to area agencies includes (U.S. DHEW, 1980b: 21155):

Monitoring, evaluating, and commenting on policies and programs affecting older persons

Assessment of needs for services in the PSA and evaluation of effectiveness of services being provided

Awarding subgrants and entering into contracts for the provision of
services under the plan
Coordination with the federal programs serving older persons

As defined in the Older Americans Act and in the rules and
regulations referred to previously, AAA's are responsible for comprehensive areawide planning for social services for the elderly.

The suggested models for needs and resource assessment, plan
development, and evaluation in this chapter should provide the
reader with a basic understanding of the planning process. Considerable attention is directed toward needs assessment because it is crucial
to effective planning and evaluation, yet it has been poorly understood and frequently neglected by planning personnel (U.S. House of
Representatives, 1977; Leinbach, 1982).

Needs Assessment and Data Sources

State and local (regional or area) needs assessments are required
under Title III of the Older Americans Act as essential components of
the planning process (U.S. DHEW, 1980b). Other agencies, public
and private, undertake needs assessments that may cover similar
topics with similar populations. Thus, the first activity in any needs
assessment is to find out what has already been done or is in the
process of being done by other agencies. A needs assessment that
provides adequate and appropriate material can be a complicated,
time-consuming, and expensive project. If several agencies requiring
data can pool financial and personnel resources, a joint effort may
result in a far superior base for planning and evaluation. Unfortunately, recent trends have shown the more typical community to have
several overlapping yet inadequate needs assessments. Some of the
reasons for this are lack of cooperation, turf protection, and impact of
special interests (Freeden and Morris, 1968).

The methods used in needs assessment are those of social research
and social epidemiology. Social epidemiology is the identification of
the following: the distribution of conditions (such as illness, crime, or
poverty) among a population, social and environmental factors
associated with increased risk of the conditions, possible causes, and
preventive or curative interventions that may reduce the rate or the
severity of the conditions.

The techniques used in social epidemiology are basically those of
social research. They include the use of available data sources (such as
reports of the U.S. Bureau of the Census, the National Center for

Health Statistics, and state agencies) and the collection of new data, usually through population sample surveys.

If a search of available publications or contacts with agencies reveal that recent analyses of demographic and statistical data have been completed, copies of appropriate reports should be obtained and used if adequate. In such cases, supplemental analysis of data and perhaps some additional interpretation may be all that is needed. Otherwise, the planning agency must start from scratch with original source documents (Wilson and Rich, 1971).

Census Data

Bureau of the Census publications contain basic demographic data for any given area. If these data are not in the form needed or are not broken down by appropriate geographic divisions, special tabulations may be ordered from the Bureau or from the data-user centers in every state. It is also possible to purchase the census computer tapes and carry out one's own tabulations and analysis.

A typical demographic analysis based on census data includes at least the following information for the planning area:[1]

Number by age and sex
Racial and ethnic composition
Marital status
Household size
Housing type and tenure (rent or own)
Income (including poverty rates)
Labor force participation
Age/youth dependency rates
Fertility ratios

It is suggested that all characteristics be crosstabulated by broad age categories even if the population of concern consists of older persons only. This crosstabulation permits the planner to examine the older population in the context of the rest of an area's population. For example, it is important to consider whether the rate of poverty is high for all age categories or just for the elderly. High potential need for services among younger persons in the area often indicates increased competition for resources and a generally lower level of tax

---

[1] The nature of data collected and the type of geographic subdivision used differ for metropolitan and nonmetropolitan areas. The reader should refer to publications of the Bureau of the Census to ascertain the nature of data available for a particular planning area.

payments, donations, and voluntary services from the non-aged segment. Similarly, high fertility rates coupled with low income for younger adults may increase competition for discretionary funds and facilities.

Vital Statistics

Data on vital statistics are available from the National Center for Vital and Health Statistics and from state vital statistics offices, which are usually housed in state health units. Categories of data that may be obtained from vital statistics reports include the following:

Fertility data—birth rates by birth weight, duration and source of prenatal care, attendance by physician, place of birth (hospital, nonhospital), age and marital status of mother, race and ethnic/minority status

Infant mortality by race and ethnic/minority status

Death rates by age, cause of death, sex, race and minority status

Average expectation of life at birth and at specific ages

Rate of natural population increase or decrease (births minus deaths per year)

Marriage rates by age, race, and minority status

Divorce rates by age, race, and minority status

Annual estimates of the population, usually by county or city, and relative importance of migration in population

The comments made about census data also apply to vital statistics data. Information covering all age categories must be examined for the planning area in order to put the implied needs in the context of the community. The presence of illegitimacy, infant and childhood mortality, homicide, or suicide rates substantially higher than those in other areas could produce competing demands for limited community resources. On the other hand, if such indicators suggest that the non-aged population is relatively well off while the aged are not, planners can document requests that a greater share of local discretionary funds be directed toward services for older persons.

Other Agency Data

Agency service statistics are available for most areas, at least on a county (sometimes on a subcounty) level. State agencies responsible for administering health and welfare programs—including Medicaid,

Title XX social services, and long-term care facility licensing—publish periodic caseload statistics. These figures can provide insights into the relative level of need as suggested by the nature and extent of services provided for the area. Some voluntary organizations such as the United Way publish similar reports. Data on Medicare, Medicaid, SSI, Title XX social services, and other programs are published by the U.S. Department of Health and Human Services (formerly the Department of Health, Education and Welfare).[2]

The sources and suggested types of data reviewed above are meant to be illustrative and not exhaustive. The examples should be sufficient to convince the reader that extensive data on indicators of problems and needs are available and should be reviewed as an important part of the planning and evaluation process.

Approaches to Data

Social Indicators

The social indicator approach involves combining data from multiple sources to compute an index of the relative status of populations. For example, the U.S. Department of Agriculture uses a combination of "median family income, educational attainment, poverty among families with employed male heads, and absence of complete plumbing in occupied housing" to provide an index of relative economic status. Other indices have been developed for health status, family status, and alienation based on data available from various sources, including census reports and vital statistics reports (Ross et al., 1979). The typical social indicator report uses a score, or index, of 100 for the national average; areas with a score above 100 are considered to be relatively better off and those with a score under 100 are relatively worse off on the characteristic being rated. Such indicators may be very useful tools for planners, but they should be considered only with other types of information.

Although the social indicator is generally used with available data, it also can be used with newly collected data or with a combination of available and new data. Table 3.1 shows some selected categories of indicators that combine new and available data. This approach was used in a national social indicator study by the Administration on

---

[2]For a summary of federal sources, see the U.S. DHEW publication *Inventory of Federal Statistical Programs Relating to Older Persons* (Washington, D.C.: U.S. Government Printing Office, 1979).

Table 3.1
Examples of Social Indicators Relating to Needs of Older Persons

Category	Components of indicators
A. Economic well-being	Welfare ratio, self-satisfaction, income, assets, debts, expenses, replacement ratio in retirement.
B. Housing quality	*Objective:* plumbing, kitchen equipment, interior temperature (and control of), availability of telephone, adequacy of lighting, number and size of rooms, tenure, security. *Subjective:* self-satisfaction, feeling of safety, degree of privacy, noise level, etc.
C. Neighborhood quality	General impression, change, suitability for older persons, availability of services such as grocery store, post office, church.
D. Health	Self-evaluation of health, number of sick days, chronic conditions, restrictions of activity, limitation of mobility, self-care, pain and suffering, depression, and anxiety.
E. Social relations and activities	Contacts with others and satisfaction with these contacts, respect received from others, meetings and activities, access to trusted person to talk to, loneliness, husband-wife roles, etc.
F. Life satisfaction	Self-evaluation, expectations for future.
G. Independence	Related to all of the above factors—general ability to carry out "normal living" in a satisfactory manner and degree of support needed in order to do so.

Aging in conjunction with state units on aging in the early 1970s (Center for Gerontological Studies and Programs, 1972). An idea underlying the use of social indicators is that the same indices be examined repeatedly over time to provide information on changes and on program impact. This was the intent of the Administration on Aging in 1971, but the longitudinal aspect was not carried out because of changes in policy and personnel.

A detailed report about these efforts, prepared for the Administration on Aging in 1973, was published by the Department of Health, Education and Welfare (1974). This document describes some of the problems associated with the use of social indicators. One of these is the often exaggerated claims and unrealistic expectations of the value of such indicators in planning and implementing service programs. Another is the ambiguity in the definition of social indicators. This confusion has been complicated by imprecise definitions of terms (such as social well-being) and the use of different definitions by different investigators (U.S. DHEW, 1974). In spite of these problems, social indicators are useful when they are used in conjunction with other information and when their limitations are taken into account.

The Informed Persons Survey Approach

An additional source of information on needs is a survey of informed persons. This type of survey may include agency administrators, senior advocacy organization leaders, and elected officials, who are asked to estimate needs or to assess program effectiveness. Although such information is needed, in itself it provides a very uncertain base for planning and evaluation. The opinions of key persons are helpful when used along with indicators derived from documents, including census, vital statistic, and agency reports, and with population survey data.

Population Surveys

The ideal needs assessment includes survey interview data from a sample designed to be representative of either the target population or the total community of which the target group is a subpopulation. In order to yield the type of information needed, the survey must be very carefully designed in terms of question content, the conduct of the interviews, and the population sampling plan. Unfortunately, most needs assessments fall short in at least one of these categories.

Although it is beyond the scope of this work to provide a detailed discussion of social survey research methods and probability sampling theory, some general points can be made. Surveys based only on data collected from program participants, people who attend community forums, or those who return a questionnaire clipped from a newspaper provide no basis for generalization. These studies simply reflect the concerns of the self-selected people who happen to participate. All too often, service plans and evaluations are founded on data collected in this manner.

Population surveys may be conducted by mail, by telephone, or through face-to-face interviews. Each approach has advantages and disadvantages. Mail surveys and phone surveys have higher refusal rates and higher item nonresponse rates than do face-to-face interviews. Mail surveys exclude those who cannot read and write, and, obviously, phone surveys do not cover those who do not have phones. While both of these methods offer advantages in cost and time, they are less likely than face-to-face interviewing to yield adequate data. An excellent discussion of the relative advantages of these techniques is presented in Seltiz et al. (1976).

All of these approaches have limitations with respect to generating samples representative of the target population. The basic representative sampling design calls for a list of all of the individuals in the target population, from which a statistically random sample may be selected. The absence of a complete list for most planning areas usually precludes this type of sampling. Several alternative sampling procedures have been developed in an effort to obtain representative samples.

Two commonly used designs are random sampling of housing units (screening selected units for the presence of older persons and gathering data on all older persons located in this manner) and geographic cluster sampling. In geographic cluster sampling, the area is divided into grids or small segments and a random selection of these small segments is drawn. Housing units are then screened, and all elderly people residing in the selected grids are included in the sample. Although neither method is as desirable as a random sample of the older population, each offers a chance for every older person in the target area to be included in the sample. These approaches are referred to by social researchers as "probability" sampling plans. Since they are based on statistical probability theory, they provide greater assurance that generalizations from samples are appropriate (Seltiz et al., 1976).

The Administration on Aging has developed a number of data collection forms to be used in needs assessments and program evaluation. While none of these may be entirely appropriate for a specific planning and service area because of regional differences, the forms do provide a pool of questions from which one can draw selected items. The use of such pools has advantages over the development of a new set of questions and permits direct comparisons with other areas. In making comparisons, the investigator must take into account possible differences in methods and in sampling. For example, mail surveys may not yield the same answers as face-to-face interviews containing the same questions.

In summary, the assessment of needs for the purpose of developing priorities, service delivery plans, and program evaluation is a complicated process. Although needs assessments are required of state and area agencies under the Older Americans Act, relatively few have been conducted in a way that provides adequate data for plan development. The combination of data collection techniques and sources reviewed here is an ideal seldom achieved in practice, but it is not beyond the capability of most planning agencies, provided suitably trained staff members are available.

Resource Assessment

Resource assessment uses a combination of new data from surveys and available data contained in directories, agency reports, and information-and-referral resource files. At most, available data may yield information on the type of service, source of funding, eligible population, number of persons served and units of service provided, fees charged, and client characteristics. The planner may need to use mail, phone, or face-to-face contacts to obtain information on the potential for increasing service, interest in pooling resources, acceptability of contracts for service, extent of waiting lists, and client processing time, as well as information on rejected applicants, reasons for rejections, and characteristics of those who were turned down. The nature and extent of information required will vary with the type of planning agency. Area agencies on aging need all of the above types of information. Planners then relate resources, agency capabilities, and eligibility requirements to the identified needs, taking into consideration the social and economic characteristics of the target group. This forms a basis for the development of plans for coordinating, pooling, and supplementing existing resources and for the development of new services to meet needs for which no resource is available.

Plan Development

Once the needs of the target population and the resources to be used in meeting these needs have been identified, service plan development can begin. For area agencies on aging, certain priorities have been legislated and must receive attention. Even so, AAA's have considerable discretion in resource allocation. Needs assessments and the results of evaluation research provide strong documentation for prioritizing plan components.

Priorities should be based on a combination of need-resource analysis, statutory requirements, agency regulations and guidelines, input from local advisers, and application of findings from prior research and program evaluations. In practice, several conditions may interfere with this rational process. Lareau and Heumann report that a nationwide survey revealed the overall quality of needs assessments to be "so low as to provide little meaningful impact to the planning process" and that "the typical needs assessment analyzed in this study may be counterproductive, resulting in misleading or incorrect findings" (1982, p. 329). Others suggest that the results of both needs assessments and evaluation research are often secondary to political, administrative, and personal considerations (Estes, 1979; Hudson and Binstock, 1976; Johnson, 1977).

Even when assessments and evaluations yield sound documentation, it is difficult to change resource allocations in established programs. Program personnel usually believe in the value of their activities and will not accept withdrawal of resources without a fight. Skillful application of public relations techniques and political pressure are effective weapons in battles over resources. Planners may find that basing priorities and allocations on documented needs and research findings can result in strained community relationships and loss of local political support. It is unlikely that this problem can be resolved totally, but educating politicians, officials, and the general public on the issue of priority development may help (Estes, 1979; Johnson, 1977).

Formulating Objectives and Action Steps

When decisions on priorities have been reached, objectives and action steps must be stated. The term *objective* refers to a relatively short-range goal that may be accomplished within a set time period; therefore, objectives must be defined in a way that permits measurement of progress. For example, one objective may be to reduce social isolation for a given target population. Social isolation may be defined as a low level of involvement in meaningful roles and interaction with other individuals and groups. The term may be further operationalized by specifying a measurement instrument that has already been used.

The means to be used in attempting to reach an objective are the bases of the *action steps* to be spelled out in the plan. Each step must state exactly what is to be done and how it is to be achieved, so that it can be replicated. Objectives and action steps provide the game plan for service delivery personnel and the framework for program monitoring and evaluation. Two broad types of program evaluation, impact and process, are discussed in some detail later. Very simply stated, *impact evaluation* assesses the extent to which program activities produce desired changes, and *process evaluation* assesses the extent to which program activities conform to the action plan (Freeman, 1980). Impact evaluation cannot be undertaken unless objectives are stated in a way that permits measurement of accomplishments. Process evaluation cannot be undertaken unless there is a precise statement of action plans, including definitions of the target population, the organizational structure, and the procedures (Estes and Freeman, 1976; Morell, 1979; Freeman, 1980).

Program Evaluation

Evaluation is an essential component of a program's cycle of planning and implementation. Rational plans build upon previous research and incorporate continuing evaluation. Consistent with this orientation, Estes and Freeman identify six activities as "critical" to effective intervention strategies. A planner must "(1) explicate the objectives of the intervention; (2) designate the target population; (3) posit a theory on how such changes can be effected; (4) develop an operational plan or treatment; (5) select organizations and practitioners to implement the program; and (6) develop a research design that permits the study of both program implementation and impact" (1976, p. 539). Rossi et al. characterize program assessment as seeking answers to five general questions: "(1) Is the intervention reaching the appropriate target population? (2) Is it being implemented in the ways specified? (3) Is it effective? (4) How much does it cost? (5) What are its costs relative to its effectiveness?" (1979, p. 21). O'Brien et al., in their definition of evaluation research, stress that such assessment must link theory and scientific methods to policies and program operation (1977). Yet it is recognized that it would be difficult for service delivery personnel to adhere to strict scientific research methods and also fulfill the expectations of the policy makers (Estes and Freeman, 1976; Morell, 1979). Morell uses the term "culture gap" in discussing differences in orientation between social science and social service. Practitioners often view theories as having little relevance to their particular programs, which they consider to be unique. Researchers emphasize similarities between different situations and seek bases for generalization. They are more concerned with long-range effects, whereas practitioners concentrate on immediate needs. Research tends to focus on change and development; agency administrators are concerned with maintaining the existing organization. Researchers attempt to answer questions, and practitioners try to help individuals (Morell, 1979). Thus, the evaluation researcher is faced with bridging the conceptual gaps between research and service, theory and practice, and science and policy.

Status of Evaluation Research

Although evaluation has been mandated for many programs (including those under the Older Americans Act and Title XX of the Social Security Act), neither policy makers nor researchers have been satisfied with the results. Agency guidelines on what constitutes accountability or program assessment are often vague and focus on monitoring and on service statistics. Monitoring activities are conducted in most agencies and typically include collection of data on client characteristics, services provided, and cost per unit of service. These data are *potentially* useful for program assessment, but Estes and Freeman conclude that "such service statistics are notoriously useless for systematic purposes for both the development of social interventions and policy analysis" (1976, p. 544). The most common problems with service statistics are systematic biases in collection and categorization, inaccuracy, and high rates of item nonreporting. These problems may stem from personnel shortages, lack of expertise, and low motivation levels of agency staff (Estes and Freeman, 1976).

McTavish reports that a high proportion of funded (mainly evaluative) research projects had serious deficiencies in research methods. He states that "between 20 and 40 percent[3] of those projects receiving research money did not include a discoverable research component in judgments made by experienced professional investigators" (1977, p. 16). Many of those which did have research components were found to have problems such as inadequate descriptions of methods, failure to build upon previous research and related literature, failure to define major concepts adequately, difficulties with sampling representativeness, lack of logical relationships between data and conclusions, and "sloppy workmanship" (McTavish, 1977). These findings support the comments of Estes and Freeman on the lack of interest, motivation, manpower, and expertise in evaluation research.

In spite of some shortcomings, evaluation research has made contributions, and its value is recognized by policy makers. Political and economic trends of the early 1980s have contributed to increased demands for accountability and documentation of program effectiveness. The 1981 *White House Conference on Aging Final Report* included the following comments and recommendations:

There are only limited data on effective modes of service delivery. There is need for evaluations of present modes of delivery of these services as well as exploration of alternate ways to enhance this service delivery.

[3]According to McTavish, the wide range in percentage occurred because some questions concerned agency interpretations of whether or not projects required research components.

The mere availability of a service does not ensure that the targeted groups will receive it or that it is an appropriate service that addresses the identified need.

The role of research in the service delivery area needs to be expanded substantially.

In the health care and social service delivery area there is a major need to examine how these services can be better organized and integrated to meet the needs of the elderly, how more efficiency can be achieved, and where more investments of effort are likely to be most effective (1981, p. 104).

The White House Conference Committee on Research concluded that aging research resources, both private and public, are inadequate. The committee recommended that funding for research and for training of researchers be expanded and that greater emphasis be placed on compiling adequate data bases, coordinating research activities, and disseminating research findings (White House Conference on Aging, 1981).

Evaluation Research

Earlier in this book, the concepts of process and impact were introduced as the two basic approaches to evaluation research. Freeman depicts process evaluation as asking whether the program was directed at the right population and whether the efforts were undertaken as stated in the action plan. Impact evaluation is pictured as asking whether the program made any difference. *Comprehensive evaluation* is defined as "one in which appropriate techniques and ideas have been utilized so that it is possible (a) to determine whether or not a programme, intervention, or treatment is carried out as planned, and (b) to assess whether or not the programme resulted in changes or modifications consistent with the intended outcome" (1980, pp. 20, 21). Thus a comprehensive evaluation is one that includes both process and impact research.

There are numerous elaborations and variations on the process-impact dichotomy, but most approaches break process and impact into various components (O'Brien et al., 1977). More extensive conceptual frameworks, of course, are useful in designing evaluation research studies, even though most can be compressed into the broad categories of process and impact. Some examples of more elaborate typologies are found in the works of Lawton, Suchman, and Rossi et al. Lawton uses the three variables of input, process, and output. He describes input variables as relating to the characteristics of clients. A question involving input might be "How do users of a particular service differ from nonusers?" Lawton's concept of process involves variables such as the nature and extent of facilities, services offered, administrative practices, and staff characteristics; output refers to the effect of the program on its target (1977). Suchman calls attention to five categories of evaluation: (1) effort (activity or input), (2) effect (result), (3) impact (adequacy of outcome), (4) efficiency (usually in terms of cost effectiveness), and (5) process (how efforts were carried out) (Suchman, 1967; Estes and Freeman, 1976). Rossi et al. identify four classes of evaluation research, which they label program planning, program monitoring, impact assessment, and process efficiency research (1979). *Program planning research* addresses questions of size, distribution, and characteristics of the target population and congruency of program design with intended goals. *Program monitoring research* assesses the extent to which the program reaches its target population and the extent to which services are delivered according to action plans. *Impact assessment research* investigates the extent to which stated goals are achieved and whether results could be explained by some process other than the program. *Process efficiency research* examines the economic costs of a program and asks if an alternative approach may constitute a more efficient use of resources (Rossi et al., 1979).

It is apparent that some terms are given somewhat different meanings by different investigators and that some "carve the pie" into different configurations. All of the above conceptual schemes, however, could be subsumed under the broadly defined concepts of process and impact.

Process Evaluation. Some critics of social service program evaluation complain that process is overemphasized to the exclusion of impact. Although there may be some validity to these complaints (mainly because of the lack of measurable objectives, lack of expertise in impact assessment, and lack of financial support for complicated impact research), the importance of process assessment cannot be denied. Evaluators must know if the action that was planned and paid for was actually carried out. In the absence of documentation that the program actually took place (process evaluation), it is useless to try to measure the impact of a program (Estes and Freeman, 1976; Freeman, 1979; Rossi et al., 1980).

A common cause of lack of measurable impact is that the programs were not implemented as planned. In Freeman's words, "If there were one major reason why so few evaluations demonstrate positive impact findings, it would surely be the failure of proper programme implementation and consequently the incorrect assumption that different groups received different treatments" (1980, p. 21). Reasons for failure to follow program plans include political considerations, incompetent or uncommitted staff, failure to identify the target population, and lack of acceptance of the program by potential clients (Freeman, 1980). Process evaluation is a way to tell policy makers, planners, and developers about what is actually taking place, and it is a way to provide insights on what works and what does not work in getting services to the target population.

Impact Evaluation. Impact evaluation implies the existence of prespecified, operationally defined objectives as well as measurable criteria of success in attaining these objectives. To measure impact, the investigator needs a research design that tests the hypothesis that observed changes are a function of the program and not the result of some other phenomenon. In social research language, impact assessment requires a causal model in which one or more independent variables (causes) are hypothesized to produce a change in the dependent variable (usually some attribute of the target population or system). Benefit-cost analysis, which is a particular type of impact assessment, also requires the assumption of a causal relationship between program efforts and benefits to the target population.

Causal Models. For reasons of economy and simplicity, the "proximal" causal approach often is used. This model focuses on a single variable that is hypothesized to affect some condition; "x causes y," or "a change in x causes a change in y." In social program evaluations, single factors seldom provide an adequate explanation, so *multi-causal models* are required. These models may be of two general types. In the first, a number of different variables acting independently affect a particular condition or behavior. In the other, a *set* of interrelated variables act together to affect a particular condition or behavior (Estes and Freeman, 1976). Multi-causal models of both types require more complex research designs and statistical analyses than do proximal causal models.

The fundamental design for testing causal relationships is the classic experiment in which two matched groups under controlled conditions are observed over time. One group is exposed to the test variable while the other is isolated from it. Any differences between the two groups after an appropriate length of time are then attributed to the test variable. Since it is virtually impossible to find two perfectly matched groups of human beings and to control the social, psychological, and physical environments in which they function, random assignment is used so that group equivalence may be inferred. But randomization is often precluded by legal, ethical, and political factors that prevent withholding services from randomly selected potential recipients. Faced with these problems, investigators sometimes use statistical manipulations to control for differences between recipient and nonrecipient groups. Such quasi-experimental designs are useful, but can lead to inappropriate conclusions. Most evaluative research on social programs relies on before-and-after measures of a single group. In this approach, it is assumed that the social system in which services are provided is relatively stable over time (Estes and Freeman, 1976; Lawton, 1977; Freeman, 1980).

System Change. Although evaluation research designs frequently imply that the social and physical environments are essentially stable, there is general agreement that this is not the case (McTavish, 1977; Lawton, 1977). Lawton uses the term "fluid" to characterize the system under study and stresses the importance of the time dimension in coping with the influences of system change. He suggests that multiple periodic measures should be used rather than simple "pre" and "post" measures (1977).

Obviously, if the number of measures increases, so will the overall costs of program assessment. In order to minimize expenses, it is recommended that intermediate measures be limited to a few carefully selected items. These items must represent the most important aspects, be cost effective, and include both process and impact levels. The desired frequency of measurements depends on program characteristics and the nature of data collected. Lawton suggests, "If the normal treatment period is twelve months, one interim evaluation would constitute an improvement, while two or three would be even better" (1977, pp. 5, 6). In general, equal intervals between measures are preferred to facilitate documentation of statistical trends, although circumstances may dictate nonequal periods. For example, measures may be timed to relate to the implementation of new programs in other agencies. Because of the possible effects of practice, "measurement fatigue," and rater bias associated with frequent contacts, data available from records should be used when possible. The use of available data also reduces costs in most instances (Lawton, 1977).

Identifying Relevant Variables

Two paradigms of variables relevant to evaluation research have been developed by Lawton and by O'Brien et al. Lawton's paradigm, used in the essay on system fluidity referred to above, emphasizes individual client assessment (subject variables) in the context of physical, personal, and social environment. O'Brien et al. focus more on community service systems, although there is some overlap in the two typologies (Lawton, 1977; O'Brien et al., 1977). Both schemes are intended to identify potentially relevant and measurable variables that are likely to operate in any social program setting. This is not to

Figure 3.1 Schematic Diagram of Sublevels of Individual Organization

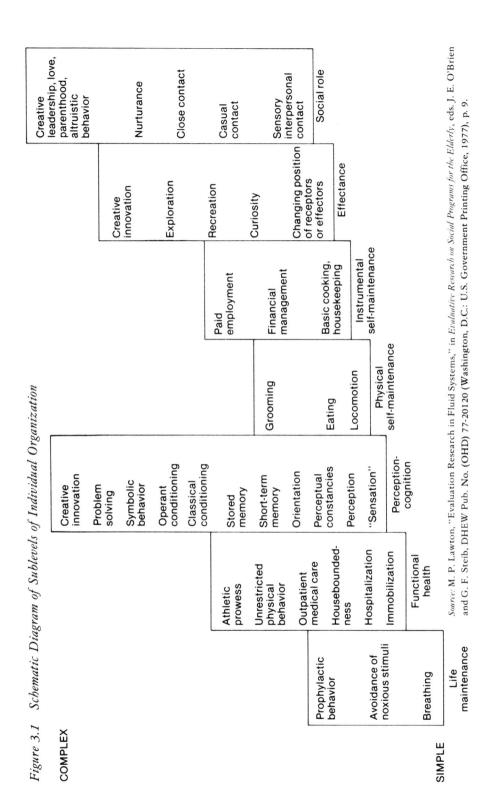

COMPLEX

Creative leadership, love, parenthood, altruistic behavior			
Nurturance			
Close contact	Creative innovation		
Casual contact	Exploration		
Sensory interpersonal contact	Recreation		
Social role	Curiosity	Paid employment	
	Changing position of receptors or effectors	Financial management	
	Effectance	Basic cooking, housekeeping	Creative innovation
		Instrumental self-maintenance	Problem solving
		Grooming	Symbolic behavior
		Eating	Operant conditioning
		Locomotion	Classical conditioning
		Physical self-maintenance	Stored memory

Short-term memory — Orientation — Perceptual constancies — Perception — "Sensation" — Perception-cognition

Athletic prowess — Unrestricted physical behavior — Outpatient medical care — Houseboundedness — Hospitalization — Immobilization — Functional health

Prophylactic behavior — Avoidance of noxious stimuli — Breathing — Life maintenance

SIMPLE

Source: M. P. Lawton, "Evaluation Research in Fluid Systems," in *Evaluative Research on Social Programs for the Elderly,* eds. J. E. O'Brien and G. F. Steib, DHEW Pub. No. (OHD) 77-20120 (Washington, D.C.: U.S. Government Printing Office, 1977), p. 9.

47

Table 3.2
Types of Variables Examined in the Evaluation of a Coordinated
Community System

	Domains			
Dimension	Coordinating agent COAG	Environment E	Organization O	Client C
History	Auspice; parent agencies; basis of inception	Nature and type of services available	History; auspice; type of service (Lefton and Rosengren)	Personal biographies
Structure	Autonomy vis-à-vis sponsor; task force composition; internal staff patterns	Local and extralocal integration (Turk, 1970)	Type of bureaucracy (Bowers, 1966); differentiation and autonomy of parts (Katz, 1968)	Problems and conditions; quality of life
Knowledge, attitudes, technology	Professionalization; staff backgrounds; ideology	Public opinion, political and economic conditions (Clark, 1965)	Complexity of technology; leadership and worker competence; staff attitudes	Abilities and training; morale and life satisfaction
Performance	Planning methodologies; coordinating methodologies	Resources available	Service delivery cost and efficiency	Changes in nutrition and health, economic standard of living (Lind & O'Brien, 1971)

Note: See original source for references.
Source: J. E. O'Brien, B. D. Lebowitz, N. Whitelaw, and R. Cherry, "Evaluating Coordinated Community Service Systems," in Evaluative Research on Social Programs for the Elderly, eds. J. E. O'Brien and G. F. Streib, DHEW Pub. No. (OHD) 77-20120 (Washington, D.C.: U.S. Government Printing Office, 1977), p. 91.

Relationships				
COAG → O	O → COAG	O ← O	O → C	C → O
Auspice; age (Rosengren and Lefton, 1970)	Number; size of history	Relational history (Aiken & Alford, 1970)	History of services available	Background and demographic characteristics
Coordinating mechanism; extent of control and authority	Similarities of structure (Levine & White, 1963); organization and specialization (Lawrence & Lorsch, 1967)	Resource needs, interorganizational context (Warren, 1967); reciprocity (Johns & Demarche, 1951)	Type of service offering, welfare, volunteer, monetary exchange	Client representation, choice of services
Policies and goals; awareness of organizations (Litwak & Hylton, 1961); professionalization	Compatability of philosophies (Miller, 1958); acceptance of COAG (Evan, 1966)	Standardization (Litwak & Hylton, 1961); intensity; domain consensus (Evan, 1966)	Information of client population; policies of organization	Knowledge of personal rights and services; welfare orientation
Interorganization communications; resource mobilization	Integration of services; coordinated activities	Agreement formalization (Leadley, 1959; Clark 1965)	Contracted agreements; availability and quality of service; turnover rate	Utilization and appraisal of services

imply that all variables must be examined for all programs. The specific items applicable to any given program depend on that program's objectives, procedures, and resources.

In the subject variable category, Lawton includes life maintenance, functional health, perception-cognition, physical self-maintenance, effectance, and social role. These classes of variables are presented in Figure 3.1 along with suggested behavioral indicators for each class. The variable classes in Figure 3.1 are ordered by level of complexity, with life maintenance at the most simple level and social role at the most complex level. A second hierarchy also appears in the listing of behavioral indicators for each variable class. For example, within the life maintenance class, prophylactic behavior is at a more complex level than breathing. Although this approach focuses on assessment of individuals, parallel systems may be used in the assessment of communities, organizations, and groups.

Subject variables occur in an environment that Lawton divides into four components: physical environment, personal environment, supra-personal environment, and social environment. Variables such as availability and type of housing, presence of facilities and resources, and accessibility of available resources fall under the physical environment heading. Personal environment involves the characteristics and behavior of close personal contacts and agency staff members. The supra-personal environment includes the characteristics and behavior of all people who are in physical proximity to the subject. Finally, the social environment involves norms and social institutions that govern behavior. In most cases, environmental variables are at the process level, although specific program objectives could relate to impact on some aspects of environment (Lawton, 1977).

The O'Brien et al. outline shown in Table 3.2 partially overlaps that of Lawton but is more elaborate and directs attention to the "coordinated community system." The purpose of this scheme is to guide research measuring "the impacts of the system on the agencies involved, the clients served and the community at large" (O'Brien et al., 1977, p. 89). This model examines the domains of (1) coordinating agent, (2) environment, (3) organization, and (4) client along the four dimensions of history, structure, knowledge and attitudes, and performance. In addition, relationships among the domains are examined along the same four dimensions. For each domain and domain relationship, variables are identified in each dimension. For example, in Table 3.2 a variable in the organization domain along the structural dimension is "service delivery cost and efficiency." A variable on the performance dimension that is identified with the relationships between the client domain and the organization domain is "utilization and appraisal of services."

The two paradigms of variables presented in the preceding discussion illustrate the complexity of research on service programs. All listed variables need not be used in all evaluation research, and the list is not exhaustive or all-inclusive. The two schemes for examining types of variables do provide a guide that may help planners and evaluators in designing process and impact studies.

Summary

Planning social services for older persons involves a set of interrelated activities. Some of these activities are necessarily sequential; others may take place simultaneously. The types of activities include assessing needs, assessing resources, obtaining input from interested parties (including service providers and advocacy groups), setting priorities and developing a plan for action based on these priorities, holding public hearings on the plan, implementing activities under the plan, and monitoring and evaluating these activities.

Because of shortages of skilled personnel, influences of local politics and special interests, ambiguity and inconsistency in goals, and inadequate financial support, the ideal in planning is rarely achieved. However, planning efforts have resulted in improved services, more effective and efficient use of resources, and the focusing of service programs on the most significant unmet needs of the older population.

As programs for older persons have developed and expanded, increasing emphasis has been placed on accountability. Monitoring systems have been developed by funding and planning agencies to check on project progress, amounts of service delivered, and characteristics of clients served. Monitoring systems contribute some of the information needed for program evaluation, at least at the process level.

Program evaluation occurs at different levels within the service delivery system. The most basic of the several classifications of levels includes the two categories of process and impact. Evaluation researchers may use different terms in referring to these levels and may divide the concepts of process and impact into components. Meaningful program assessment cannot take place if objectives and action steps are not stated clearly and in a way that permits measurement of progress. Impact evaluation requires clear documentation of process and application of research designs that test causal hypotheses. System change over time is recognized as a factor that may cloud issues in documenting cause-and-effect relationships.

Although the track record of social service program evaluation efforts has been poor, the importance and potential of evaluation are recognized. Social and economic conditions of the 1980s dictate greater attention to evaluation research as a basis for deciding how to obtain the greatest benefit from scarce resources.

References

Beattie, W. M., Jr. "Aging and the Social Services." In *Handbook of Aging and the Social Services*, eds. R. H. Binstock and E. Shanas, pp. 619–642. New York: Van Nostrand Reinhold Co., 1976.

Binstock, R. H., and M. A. Levin. "The Political Dilemmas of Intervention Policies." In *Handbook of Aging and the Social Services*, eds. R. H. Binstock and E. Shanas, pp. 511–535. New York: Van Nostrand Reinhold Co., 1976.

Center for Gerontological Studies and Programs, University of Florida, and Aging Studies Program, University of South Florida. *Social Indicators to Measure the Conditions of Life of Florida's Older People.* Gainesville, FL: Center for Gerontological Studies, 1972.

Estes, C. L. "Barriers to Effective Community Planning for the Elderly." *The Gerontologist* 13 (1973): 178–183.

_____. "Community Planning for the Elderly: A Study of Goal Displacement." *Journal of Gerontology* 29 (1974): 684–691.

_____. *The Aging Enterprise*. San Francisco: Jossey-Bass Publishers, 1979.

Estes, C. L., and H. E. Freeman. "Strategies of Design and Research for Intervention." In *Handbook of Aging and the Social Sciences*, eds. R. H. Binstock and E. Shanas, pp. 536–560. New York: Van Nostrand Reinhold Co., 1976.

Florida Department of Health and Rehabilitative Services. *Proposed Comprehensive Annual Services Program Plan for Title XX—Social Security Act.* Tallahassee, FL: State of Florida, 1980a.

_____. *State Plan on Aging under Title III of the Older Americans Act for Florida, 1981–83.* Tallahassee, FL: State of Florida, 1980b.

Freeden, B. J., and R. Morris. *Urban Planning and Social Policy.* New York: Basic Books, 1968.

Freeman, H. E. "The Present Status of Evaluation Research." In *Evaluating Social Action Projects*, Division for Socioeconomic Analysis, pp. 9–50. Paris, France: UNESCO, 1980.

Harbert, A. S., and H. Ginsberg. *Human Services for Older Adults: Concepts and Skills.* Belmont, CA: Wadsworth Publishing Co., 1979.

Harris, L., and Associates. *The Myth and Reality of Aging in America.* Washington, D.C.: The National Council on the Aging, 1975.

Hendricks, J., and C. D. Hendricks. *Aging in Mass Society*, 2nd ed. Cambridge, MA: Winthrop Publishers, 1981.

Hudson, R. B. "The Graying of the Federal Budget and Its Consequences for Old Age Policy." *The Gerontologist* 18, 5 (1978): 428–450.

_____, and R. H. Binstock. "Political Systems and Aging." In *Handbook of Aging and the Social Sciences*, eds. R. H. Binstock and E. Shanas, pp. 369–400. New York: Van Nostrand Reinhold Co., 1976.

Johnson, H. "Statement by Dr. Harold Johnson." In *Older Americans Program Oversight*, U.S. House of Representatives, Select Committee on Aging. Washington, D.C.: U.S. Government Printing Office, 1977.

Kendig, H. L., and R. Warren. "The Adequacy of Census Data in Planning and Advocacy for the Elderly." *The Gerontologist* 16 (1976): 392–396.

Kent, D., R. Kastenbaum, and S. Sherwood, eds. *Research, Planning, and Action for the Elderly*. New York: Behavioral Publications, 1972.

Lareau, L. S., and L. F. Heumann. "The Inadequacy of Needs Assessments of the Elderly." *The Gerontologist* 22 (1982): 324–330.

Lawton, M. P. "Evaluation Research in Fluid Systems." In *Evaluative Research on Social Programs for the Elderly*, eds. J. E. O'Brien and G. F. Streib, DHEW Pub. No. (OHD) 77-20120, pp. 5–15. Washington, D.C.: U.S. Government Printing Office, 1977.

Lebowitz, B. D. "Old Age and Family Functioning." *Journal of Gerontological Social Work* 1 (Winter, 1978): 111–118.

Leinbach, R. M. "Alternatives to the Face-to-Face Interview for Collecting Gerontological Needs Assessment Data." *The Gerontologist* 22, 1 (1982): 78–82.

McTavish, D. G. "Macro-Variance and Micro-Variance: Some Thoughts on Design Strategies in Evaluative Research." In *Evaluative Research on Social Programs for the Elderly*, eds. J. E. O'Brien and G. F. Streib, pp. 16–23. Washington, D.C.: U.S. Government Printing Office, 1977.

Morell, J. A. *Program Evaluation in Social Research*. New York: Pergamon Press, 1979.

Morris, R., and R. H. Binstock. *Feasible Planning for Social Change*. New York: Columbia University Press, 1966.

Morris, R., and M. Rein. "Emerging Patterns in Community Planning." In *Urban Planning and Social Policy*, eds. B. J. Freeden and R. Morris, pp. 23–38. New York: Basic Books, 1968.

National Retired Teachers Association/American Association of Retired Persons. *Proposals for a National Policy on Aging*. Washington, D.C.: NRTA-AARP, 1971.

O'Brien, J. E., B. D. Lebowitz, N. Whitelaw, and R. Cherry. "Evaluating Coordinated Community Service Systems." In *Evaluative Research on Social Programs for the Elderly*, eds. J. E. O'Brien and G. F. Streib, DHEW Pub. No. (OHD) 77-20120, pp. 81–105. Washington, D.C.: U.S. Government Printing Office, 1977.

Ross, P. J., B. Herman, and F. K. Hines. *Indicators of Social Well-Being for U.S. Counties*, Rural Development Research Report No. 10. Washington, D.C.: U.S. Department of Agriculture, May, 1979.

Rossi, P. H., H. E. Freeman, and S. R. Wright. *Evaluation: A Systematic Approach*. Beverly Hills, CA: Sage Publications, 1979.

Seltiz, C., M. Jahoda, M. Deutsch, and S. Cook. *Research Methods in Social Relations*, rev. ed. New York: Holt, Rinehart, and Winston, 1976.

Shanas, E. "The Elderly as a Social Support System in Old Age." *The Gerontologist* 19 (1979): 169–174.

Sherwood, S. "Social Science and Action Research." In *Research Planning and Action for the Elderly*, eds. D. P. Kent, R. Kastenbaum, and S. Sherwood, pp. 70–96. New York: Behavioral Publications, 1972.

Suchman, E. *Evaluative Research*. New York: Russell Sage Foundation, 1967.

U.S. Bureau of the Census. "Social and Economic Characteristics of the Older Population: 78." *Current Population Reports*, Series P-23, No. 85. Washington, D.C.: U.S. Government Printing Office, 1979.

U.S. Department of Health and Human Services, Administration on Aging. "Older Americans Month May, 1981, Information Package." Washington, D.C.: AoA, 1981.

_____, National Advisory Council on Aging. *Our Future Selves*, DHEW Pub. No. (OHDS) 78-1443. Washington, D.C.: U.S. Government Printing Office, 1978.

_____, Administration on Aging. *Indicators of the Status of the Elderly in the United States,* DHEW Pub. No. (OHDS) 74-20080. Washington, D.C.: U.S. Government Printing Office, 1974.

_____, Social and Rehabilitation Service. "Social Services Programs for Individuals and Families: Title XX of the Social Security Act." *Federal Register*, Vol. 42, January 31, 1977, pp. 5842–5861.

_____, Administration on Aging. *Inventory of Federal Statistical Programs Relating to Older Persons*. Washington, D.C.: U.S. Government Printing Office, 1979a.

_____, Administration on Aging. *Older Americans Act of 1965 as Amended: History and Related Acts*, DHEW Pub. No. (OHDS) 79-20170. Washington, D.C.: U.S. Government Printing Office, 1979b.

_____, Administration on Aging. *Facts about Older Americans, 1978*, DHEW Pub. No. (OHDS) 79-20006. Washington, D.C.: U.S. Government Printing Office, 1980a.

_____, Office of Human Development Services. "Grants for State and Community Programs on Aging: Rules and Regulations." *Federal Register*, Vol. 45, No. 63, March 31, 1980b, pp. 21126–21166.

U.S. House of Representatives, Select Committee on Aging. *Older American Programs Oversight*. Washington, D.C.: U.S. Government Printing Office, 1977.

Wilson, A. J. E., III. "An Introduction to Public Health Program Evaluation." Harrisburg, PA: Pennsylvania Department of Health, 1967.

_____. "Implementation and Evaluation." In *The Proceedings of the Workshop on Rural Gerontology Research in the Northeast*, eds. D. A. Watkins and C. O. Crawford, pp. 124–134. Ithaca, NY: Northeast Center for Rural Development, 1978.

_____, and T. A. Rich. "Collection and Application of Demographic Data in Program Planning and Development." In *Proceedings of a Seminar on Research Communications and Utilization in Aging*. Kansas City, MO: Administration on Aging, 1971.

Chapter

4

Access Services

Because of physical and social isolation, lack of transportation, lack of understanding, and lack of familiarity with agency procedures, many older persons do not obtain needed services. In some cases, the result may be unnecessary institutionalization; in others, the quality of life is substantially less than what is possible. Historically, mechanisms intended to bring the isolated, perhaps uninterested and uninformed potential client into the service delivery system were inconsistent and spotty. In the 1960s, efforts designed specifically for this function were formalized and evaluated in response to the requirements of newly legislated social service programs. The term *access services* is used to group these activities.

Problems of access involve not only physical barriers, but also psychological and cultural barriers that limit or prevent the delivery of needed services (Perlman and Gurin, 1972). The Administration on Aging defines access services as "services such as transportation, outreach, information and referral, escort, individual needs assessment, and service management" (U.S. DHEW, 1980: 21154). The 1978 amendments to the Older Americans Act made access services a priority area under state and area plans developed in response to the act. Specifically, the act stated that each area plan

> shall . . . provide assurance that at least 50 percent of the amount allotted for Part B (community services) will be expanded for the delivery of services associated with access to services (transportation, outreach, and information and referral); in-home services (homemaker and home health aide, visiting and telephone reassurance, and chore maintenance); and legal services; and that some funds will be expended for each such category of services (U.S. DHEW, 1979a: 27).

Although the 1978 legislation required that at least half of each area's allocation be spent on priority services, it did not specify the proportion of those funds to be used for any one of the categories— only that expenditures had to be made in each area of service. Amendments in 1981 retained these priority areas, but dropped the 50 percent or more requirement (U.S. Congress, 1982). Access services are provided by government and voluntary agencies and by informal providers (family, neighbors, and churches).

In the review that follows, those services concerned with reaching potential clients and with increasing acceptance are discussed first. Then the services that are involved in defining more precisely the client's needs and in arranging for service to be delivered (assessment and service management) are described, followed by the services that bring the client and the provider together physically (transportation and escort).

Information and Referral and Outreach

Historically, communities have provided centralized information on services and referral to appropriate service providers under a variety of auspices (Institute for Interdisciplinary Studies, 1975; New, 1962; Carter and Webber, 1966). Attention to information-and-referral contacts intensified with the war on poverty and with the expansion of social service programs in the 1960s. Federal agencies that have operated information-and-referral components include the Department of Agriculture, the Veterans Administration, the Department of Labor, the U.S. Public Health Service, the Administration for Public Service, the Office of Education, the General Services Administration, the Department of Energy, the Social Security Administration, the Rehabilitation Services Administration, and the Administration on Aging (U.S. DHEW, 1979). An Interdepartmental Task Force on Information and Referral (I and R) was created in 1975 to assess existing federal information-and-referral resources and to develop a plan to coordinate them. This task force defined *I and R* as "a systematic approach to link people in need of services to appropriate resources" and identified the essential components of an I-and-R service as staff, resource inventory, communications, linkage, and funding (U.S. DHEW, undated). The Institute of Interdisciplinary Studies suggested that information-and-referral services have "different forms, varying from highly organized, well-staffed, autonomous centers to the dispensing of information and advice by various direct service components, such as hospitals, welfare offices, educational institutions, etc." (Institute for Interdisciplinary Studies, 1971: 1).

For the purposes of this text, an I-and-R service provider is defined as an identifiable agency or separate component of an agency that does the following: develops and continually updates an inventory of resources in its service area; informs the general public about the resources and the I-and-R service; maintains visibility, accessibility, and acceptability to potential users; provides for telephone and walk-in contacts; has a staff skilled in communicating with diverse segments of the population, including ethnic minorities; provides information on specific concerns of users; makes referrals to agencies as indicated; follows up with users and agencies to ascertain the outcome of referrals; and maintains records of contacts and actions taken.

The Older Americans Act requires the provision of I-and-R services in all planning and service areas. Prior to fiscal year 1982, programs under Title XX of the Social Security Act also required I and R. The Omnibus Budget Reconciliation Act of 1981 incorporated activities formerly funded under Title XX under the Social Services Block Grant Program. Under block grants, I-and-R services may be funded at the discretion of state governments. In some cases, local agencies such as the United Way contract to provide I-and-R services that meet the needs of several agencies while conforming to statutory requirements. A few states have regional or statewide telephone I-and-R systems with toll-free lines. Some local programs also conduct *outreach* activities, which, while they include I and R, are broader and a bit different in orientation. Outreach workers may go into the community, make home visits, and establish a trust relationship as well as provide information and referral.

Outreach programs are intended to inform people of available services, help identify needs, and overcome barriers or resistance to utilization of needed services. In a sense, outreach may be considered a part of information and referral, but it is generally categorized separately. I-and-R programs assume that the person who has a problem or needs a service will initiate contact if he or she knows whom to contact. Outreach operates under the assumption that people may not know that services exist, may not realize that they need services, or may not want to contact either the I-and-R service or the potential service provider because of personal, cultural, or other factors (Perlman and Gurin, 1972; Booth, 1968). Outreach programs have been especially effective in working with isolated and alienated populations, including the rural aged, minoritites, and social dropouts (Booth, 1968; Foley, 1976; Northeast Center for Rural Development, 1978; Newsome, 1977; U.S. DHEW, 1976a).

The title of Booth's booklet, "Reaching Out to the Hard to Reach," is descriptive of outreach. How does one locate those who by definition are physically, socially, culturally, and psychologically isolated, alienated, and out of contact with the mainstream of society? In the section on needs assessment earlier in this volume (Chapter 3), the use of demographic and other available data is emphasized. These data can help the outreach program identify geographic areas (census enumeration districts or tracts and city blocks) that contain concentrations of "high-risk" individuals. These areas may have high proportions of minorities or single-person housing units, or they may be areas in which houses are geographically isolated (Wilson, 1972). Thus the outreach program can target efforts for neighborhoods where there are likely to be people in need of service.

The outreach worker attempts to break down the resistance of potential clients by "legitimizing" the service provider, by providing information, and by reassuring people that they will be treated with respect and dignity by agency staff (Fannin, 1971; Foley, 1976). Because potential clients must accept workers and develop rapport with them, outreach workers are sometimes recruited from the target population. If the target population contains many older blacks or Hispanics, efforts are made to use black and Hispanic outreach workers who know the neighborhood and who will not receive automatic rejection by the hard-to-reach (Wilson, 1972). Although some programs require that the worker be trained in social casework or gerontology, the "indigenous nonprofessional" approach has been used effectively. However, care must be used in the recruiting, screening, and training of nonprofessional outreach workers. A worker who misinforms or gets carried away in overserving the client may do more harm than good. The nonprofessional outreach worker can link the hard-to-reach client with an agency, but rarely has the skills needed to assess the client's problems and resources and to arrange for provision of services. These activities fall under the category of service (or case) management.

Service Management

Service management functions are usually carried out by professional workers with degrees in social work, gerontology, or a related field. Agencies that employ service managers provide or arrange for in-service training specifically related to the functions of the agency. Although the concept of service management was formally introduced to the aging network only recently, it has been used under a number of names by social caseworkers, rehabilitation counselors, and others for many years (U.S. DHEW, 1976b; Perlman and Gurin, 1972; Loeb, 1979). A manual for service management prepared for the Pennsylvania Office for the Aging defines service management as:

> a process which is an extention of the AAA's mandate to coordinate service for the elderly. It is done for and with a selected subset of clients and is for the purpose of providing access to the entire services system and ensuring the coordinated delivery of multiple services to individual clients. Basic to service management is an initial broad-based assessment of the client's needs. In addition, the service management process involves ensuring that: a service plan is written which considers all available service solutions; the client is actually connected to service; and the progress of the client is reexamined and the process updated at regular intervals (Philadelphia Geriatric Center, 1977: 8).

The steps in service management are (1) assessment, (2) development of a service plan, (3) arrangement of service, (4) follow-up, and (5) reassessment. Because of the need for uniform and adequate records concerning each step in the process, most agencies adopt standard forms for case recording. Assessment includes examination of both needs and resources in multiple areas, such as physical health, activities of daily living, social supports, physical environment, mental status, and economic status. The service plan is made through input and agreement of both the client and the service manager. It includes a summary of problems, a set of goals, and specific services to be provided. It may also include provision of services by family or neighbors along with services from one or more agencies. The service manager follows up to make certain that the plan is carried out and that the goals are being met. Periodic reassessment of the client is included as part of the service plan (Philadelphia Geriatric Center, 1977).

Although the preceding description of service management is specific to the Older Americans Act program in Pennsylvania, the underlying concepts are applicable in other contexts. Service management is a means of improving services to people in any setting— private home, group home, or institution.

Transportation and Escort

Transportation problems of older persons have been the subject of numerous conferences and workshops. The issues paper of the 1971 White House Conference on Aging stated that available systems were not meeting the needs of older people because of (1) high cost,

(2) limited geographic service areas on the part of public transit, (3) the orientation of facilities and transportation networks toward the private automobile, and (4) transportation system designs that pose maneuverability and orientation problems (White House Conference on Aging, 1971a). Thus transportation is interrelated with other programs through design and location considerations as well as economic considerations (Lowy, 1979; White House Conference on Aging, 1971a). Low-income individuals often reside in areas isolated from needed facilities and either unserved or underserved by public transit systems.

Planners for the 1981 White House Conference on Aging recognized that transportation issues had not changed substantially since the 1971 conference. Major concerns expressed in a pre–White House Conference symposium were the elderly's lack of access to facilities, the impact of crime and associated fear of using public transit, high energy costs, and either higher insurance rates or lack of insurance coverage for older drivers (Donahue, 1979). Although attention to these concerns had increased during the 1970s and numerous programs were initiated through demonstration and community service projects under the Older Americans Act, transportation remained a major concern at the 1981 White House Conference on Aging.

Prevost suggests that most senior adults develop mobility problems at some point. Age-related sensory changes, such as declining sight and hearing, along with other impairments, including arthritis and cardiovascular disease, limit both the ability to drive and the ability to use mass transit systems designed for younger persons (Prevost, 1976). For the majority of older persons, difficulties in maintaining and operating a private automobile do not develop until late in life. The relatively young old people (under age 75) usually continue to own and drive cars, but increasing costs deter use. New fuel-efficient cars are priced beyond the means of many older persons. Therefore, the elderly tend to keep older autos, which are likely to be gas-guzzlers and need frequent repairs.

Atchley reports that older persons also tend to avoid the use of public transportation systems (1980). He suggests that systems are designed to get people back and forth to work and that the travel needs of the elderly are seldom a concern of the designers and operators of such programs. Atchley divides older people into two broad categories—those who can use present means and those who cannot. He estimates that about 46 percent of persons age 65 and over have little or no difficulty with transportation. The 54 percent who do have problems are those who could use public systems but cannot afford to, those who need to be picked up and returned to their homes, and those who live where there is no public transportation. It is estimated that about ten million older people cannot afford available transportation and that this lack of transportation severely limits their independence and social involvement (Atchley, 1980).

Specialized Programs for the Aged

Estes reports that the two highest ranked needs in a recent survey of area agencies on aging were transportation and income assistance. Yet the area agencies provided virtually no income assistance and very little transportation assistance in absolute dollar terms (Estes, 1979). A study by Westat in fiscal year 1976, however, showed that transportation ranked first in the number of projects funded through area agencies (1978). Obviously the key to this contradiction is found in the phrase "in absolute dollar terms." AAA budgets are small compared to the costs of needed services; the AAA transportation projects are high in number but low in resources and extent of service.

Projects funded through AAA's and Title XX (social services provision of the Social Security Act) focus on essentials. That is, most older persons can obtain transportation to a doctor, dentist, senior center, nutrition project, or grocery store. These are the priority areas for most programs; however, increasing costs have caused cutbacks in even these components. Transportation for visiting family and friends, for social and cultural activities, and for recreation (other than that provided at senior centers and nutrition sites) is extremely limited. The informal system of family and friends does help to fill some of these needs, but the pride and sense of dignity of many older people prevent them from asking others for rides (Atchley, 1980; Estes, 1979).

Mass Transit

A variety of approaches have been used in transportation projects for the elderly. Design aspects that facilitate access by the aged and the handicapped have been included in newer public transit systems and are required under Urban Mass Transit Act (UMTA) guidelines (Beattie, 1976; Estes, 1979). Although these factors increase accessibility for some older persons, they fall far short of meeting the needs of the majority. Several reasons are cited to explain why the elderly do not often use the newer urban transit systems. Foremost among these is the fear of crime. Older persons, particularly those who appear to be frail and vulnerable, are favorite targets of muggers, pickpockets, pursesnatchers, and con artists. A second reason is the lack of familiarity with the automated systems and their potentially confusing maze of corridors, escalators, and elevators. Trying to get onto the right vehicle when it is going in the right direction can pose overwhelming problems for the person with vision, hearing, and ambulation limitations. Computerized fare systems and fares that vary by time of day and day of week also cause feelings of confusion and insecurity in some people. Frequently, the machine-dispensed fare cards are difficult to read and understand. Therefore, the 1979 symposium referred to previously recommended increased emphasis on making mass transit systems more usable for older persons (Donahue, 1979).

A number of innovations have been introduced to increase transportation availability and acceptability. The most common are (1) reduced fares for those capable of using public transportation, (2) public subsidies for transportation including use of taxicabs, (3) use of volunteers driving their own cars, (4) pickup and delivery service by nonprofit senior centers and nutrition sites, and (5) use of church buses. Because of costs, insurance considerations, and scheduling, most of these programs fall short of meeting general transportation needs, although they do enable the elderly to participate in specific activities (Atchley, 1980; Estes, 1979; Beattie, 1976).

The Department of Transportation operates four programs intended to assist the elderly: capital assistance for public sponsors, capital assistance for private nonprofit sponsors, fare supplements or reductions, and capital and operating assistance for the elderly. Only a small proportion (about 2 percent) of the department's budget has been earmarked for the needs of the aged and the handicapped, however (Estes, 1979). The provisions for reduced fares during off hours required by UMTA have been of some help to those older persons who are able to use mass transit programs, but, as stated above, many cannot or do not use such programs.

Thus, even though progress has been made, transportation remains a critical area for program development. The special needs of the rural elderly have not been discussed in detail here, but it should be obvious that long distances, low population density, scarcity of facilities and resources, and economic factors exacerbate problems experienced by the urban elderly and necessitate greater initiative and innovation on the part of service providers (Wilson, 1981).

Escort Services

Escort services arrange for people to accompany older individuals to and from their destinations. In some communities, formal escort services are limited to trips for such essentials as health care and social services. A person unable to use public transportation alone may do so with the special assistance and reassurance provided by the escort. The informal system of family, neighbors, church members, and others also provides services in this category (U.S. DHEW, 1980).

Escorts may be needed by people with sensory or ambulation impairments, by those who are socially and psychologically insecure, and by those who are unable to speak English. Organized volunteers and paid escorts are used, depending on local resources and philosophy. In some cases, escorts drive their own cars or agency-owned vehicles. In other instances, the escorts assist in the use of public transportation or simply walk with the older person. Escorts often help their clients with shopping, with participation in social and cultural activities, and with visiting friends or relatives (Harbert and Ginsberg, 1979; Booth, 1968; Foley, 1976).

Summary

Because of isolation, alienation, lack of understanding, or insecurity, substantial numbers of older people fail to use available services. In order to bring the elderly with needs together with people in a position to help, the category of services referred to as "access" has evolved. Access services are of three types: those which inform persons of services and reduce resistance to using the services; those which assess specific needs, develop a plan, and arrange for service; and those which bring the client and the service provider together physically.

The first category includes information-and-referral (I and R) programs, which give out information on services and direct inquiring clients to appropriate providers. It also includes outreach, which has similar functions but involves seeking out those who, for a variety of reasons, are unable or unwilling to initiate contact with either an I-and-R service or a potential service provider. Outreach operations are often directed toward high-risk populations that have been identified through demographic analyses and needs assessments.

The second category consists of case management, or service management, activities. These activities include carrying out individual assessments, developing an individualized service plan with client participation, initiating service delivery under the plan, and following up at intervals to check on progress and to reassess the client's needs.

The third category, which involves bringing the client and the service provider together, is transportation and escort services. Many of the very old (age 75 and above) do not own or cannot drive an automobile and depend on public transit, special transportation programs, and rides with friends, neighbors, or volunteers. Improvements in transportation through public and private resources have been made, but high costs and geographic distances continue to limit these services. Sensory and physical impairments and psychological insecurity often limit older people's use of public facilities. Escort services (the provision of a person to accompany and assist a vulnerable older person) have proven to be of value.

Access services have been in the priority group under the Older Americans Act and related legislation for some time. Most areas of the country have at least limited services in all three of the access categories mentioned above. However, transportation and escort services are often restricted to use in connection with "essential" services and are concentrated in relatively small geographic areas. Rapidly rising energy costs and general inflation have prevented the ideal from being achieved and have necessitated innovative efforts and greater reliance on the informal system.

References

Atchley, R. C. *The Social Forces in Later Life*, 3rd ed. Belmont, CA: Wadsworth Publishing Co., 1980.

Beattie, W. M., Jr. "Aging and the Social Services." In *Handbook of Aging and the Social Sciences*, eds. R. H. Binstock and E. Shanas, pp. 619–642. New York: Van Nostrand Reinhold Co., 1976.

Booth, F. E. "Reaching Out to the Hard to Reach Older Person." San Francisco: San Francisco Senior Center, 1968.

Carter, H. W., and I. L. Webber. *The Aged and Chronic Disease.* Jacksonville, FL: Florida State Board of Health, 1966.

Donahue, W. T. *Symposium Findings: White House Conferences as Agents of Social Change.* Washington, D.C.: International Center for Social Gerontology, 1979.

Estes, C. L. *The Aging Enterprise.* San Francisco: Jossey-Bass Publishers, 1979.

Fannin, R. *Final Report: Country Gathering, A Nutrition Demonstration Project.* Olive Hill, KY: Northeast Kentucky Area Development Council, 1971.

Federal Council on the Aging. *The Interrelationships of Benefit Programs for the Elderly. Appendix I, Handbook of Federal Programs Benefiting Older Americans.* Washington, D.C.: U.S. Government Printing Office, 1975.

Foley, L. M., ed. *Stand Close to the Door.* Sacramento, CA: California State University, 1976.

Gilbert, F. B., and the I.C.H.R. Staff. *Information and Referral: How to Do It*, DHEW Pub. No. (OHDS) 77-20400. Washington, D.C.: U.S. Government Printing Office, 1975.

Harbert, A. S., and L. H. Ginsberg. *Human Services for Older Adults: Concepts and Skills.* Belmont, CA: Wadsworth Publishing Co., 1979.

Institute for Interdisciplinary Studies. *Information and Referral Centers: A Functional Analysis.* Washington, D.C.: American Rehabilitation Foundation, 1971. (Also reprinted by U.S. Department of Health, Education and Welfare, DHEW Pub. No. (OHD) 75-20235. Washington, D.C.: U.S. Government Printing Office, 1975.)

Institute of Public Administration. *Planning Handbook: Transportation Services for the Elderly*, DHEW Pub. No. (OHD) 76-20280. Washington, D.C.: U.S. Government Printing Office, 1975.

Lawton, M. P. *Environment and Aging.* Monterey, CA: Brooks/Cole Publishing Co., 1980.

Loeb, M. B. "Gerontology Is Not a Profession—the Oldest or the Youngest." In *Gerontology in Higher Education*, eds. H. L. Sterns, E. F. Ansello, B. M. Sprouse, and R. Layfield-Faux, pp. 34–36. Belmont, CA: Wadsworth Publishing Co., 1979.

Lowy, L. *Social Work with the Aged.* New York: Harper and Row Publishers, 1979.

New, P. K. "An Information Service for the Aging." *Geriatrics* 17 (1962): 609–614.

Newsome, B. L., ed. *Insights on the Minority Elderly.* Washington, D.C.: National Center on Black Aged, 1977.

Northeast Center for Rural Development. *The Proceedings of the Workshop on Rural Gerontology Research in the Northeast.* Ithaca, NY: Cornell University, 1978.

Perlman, R., and A. Gurin. *Community Organization and Social Planning.* New York: John Wiley and Sons, 1972.

Philadelphia Geriatric Center. *A Service Management Manual* (working draft). Philadelphia: Philadelphia Geriatric Center, 1977.

Prevost, T. E. *Aging: Senior Impact: Handbook on Aging and Senior Adult Ministries.* Atlanta, GA: Home Mission Board, Southern Baptist Convention, 1976.

U.S. Congress, Committee on Education and Labor. *Compilation of the Older Americans Act of 1965 and Related Provisions of Law as Amended through December 29, 1981.* Washington, D.C.: U.S. Government Printing Office, 1982.

U.S. Department of Health and Human Services, Administration on Aging. *Guide to AoA Programs*, DHHS Pub. No. (OHDS) 80-20176. Washington, D.C.: U.S. Government Printing Office, 1980.

_____, Administration on Aging. "Older Americans Month May, 1981, Information Package." Washington, D.C.: U.S. Government Printing Office, 1981.

U.S. Department of Health, Education and Welfare, Administration on Aging. *Report of the Interdepartmental Task Force on Information and Referral.* DHHS Pub. No. (OHDS) 79-20045. Washington, D.C.: U.S. Government Printing Office, 1979.

_____, Administration on Aging. "Grants for State and Community Programs on Aging: Rules and Regulations." *Federal Register*, Vol. 45, No. 63, March 31, 1980, pp. 21126–21166.

_____, Administration on Aging. *I and R Guide.* Washington, D.C.: U.S. Government Printing Office, undated.

U.S. Senate, Special Committee on Aging. *The Proposed Fiscal Year 1983 Budget: What It Means for Older Americans.* Washington, D.C.: U.S. Government Printing Office, 1982.

Westat, Inc. *Evaluation of the Area Planning and Social Services Program (July 1974–June 1976), Vol. I: Focus on Changes in Services to Older Persons.* Rockville, MD: Westat, 1978.

White House Conference on Aging. *Background and Issues: Transportation.* Washington, D.C.: White House Conference on Aging, 1971a.

_____. *Delegate Workbook on Transportation.* Washington, D.C.: White House Conference on Aging, 1971b.

Wilson, A. J. E., III. *Final Report on Delivery of Service to the Tampa Model City Aged.* Tampa, FL: University of South Florida, 1972.

_____. "Review of Research on the Rural Aged." Paper presented at annual meeting of the Southern Gerontological Society, Atlanta, Georgia, 1981.

Chapter

5

Income Maintenance and Employment Services

It has been suggested that many of the public service needs of older persons as well as their problems of isolation, alienation, and insecurity could be prevented or reduced if adequate income were provided now and assured for the future (White House Conference on Aging, 1971d). The income background and issues paper for the 1971 White House Conference on Aging referred to income as "one of the most powerful forces which affect the life of a person or that of a family. In order to achieve a sense of economic and psychological well-being, a certain adequate level of income as well as assurance that such income will continue are of fundamental concern to everyone" (1971c: 5).

Although the old adage "money doesn't buy happiness" is often quoted, evidence from social research shows that, as a group, people with adequate income are better off in measures of life satisfaction, sense of psychological well-being, health, and morale (White House Conference on Aging, 1971c; Schultz, 1980b; U.S. DHEW, 1977b; McCoy and Brown, 1978; U.S. House of Representatives, 1977). Congressman Claude Pepper, an outspoken advocate for the aged, testified at a Congressional hearing that "poverty cannot be measured in statistical tables. It must be measured in the suffering exacted in human lives. It is impossible to quantify the human isolation experienced by elderly persons who cannot afford either a phone or bus fare, a hearing aid, or a pair of eyeglasses, or a set of dentures" (U.S. House of Representatives, 1977). Pepper did recognize, however, that "money isn't everything." For example, giving older people money to purchase needed services and goods will accomplish little unless the needed goods and services are available. He mentioned specifically the inadequacies in both quality and quantity of housing, health care, and transportation services.

Income Level and Adequacy

It is widely accepted that the income of most older persons in the United States is inadequate. Because substantial improvements were made in the income levels of the elderly during the 1970s, some critics suggest that the picture of income inadequacy could be a fallacy or a stereotype based on overgeneralization and imprecise concepts. Schulz makes the point that "there is no such thing as the collective aged: the aged are as diverse as the population itself; and this is just as true for economic status as it is for other areas" (Schulz, 1980a). Since the aged are such a heterogeneous group, no one policy or program can address their economic needs. There are great differences in the definition of "adequate" income by agencies, economic analysts, advocacy groups, and individuals. Income adequacy is also affected by whether the person is retired, partially retired, or still working; the extent of accumulated assets; and the age of the older person. It has been found that the very old have lower incomes, but they also have lower expectations and a lifestyle that does not demand as high an income. In general, recent retirees have much higher incomes than those who retired at an earlier time. Recent retirees receive Social Security benefits based on higher earnings and are more likely to have private pensions (Schulz, 1980a).

Thus, while indices such as the federal government's "poverty level" and the Bureau of the Census reports on income level show the elderly to be a disadvantaged group, there is great variance within this group, and various measures of poverty may be misleading. According to the Administration on Aging, about one-fifth of the males and approximately 8 percent of females age 65 and over were in the labor force in 1978 (U.S. DHHS, 1980a). The young old are more likely to be working than the old old, although trends over the past 20 years have been toward earlier retirement. The Bureau of Census reported that for the year 1976, median family income for families headed by a person age 65 or over was $7850 if the head did not work, $10,669 if the head of the household worked part time for more than half of the year, and $16,000 if the head of household worked full time for more than half of the year (U.S. Bureau of Census, 1979).

The income of the older population also varies considerably by sex and by family status. In 1977, families whose head of household was 65 or over had a median income of $9110, whereas unrelated individuals (not in families) had a median income of $3829–$3088 for females and $5526 for males (U.S. Bureau of Census, 1979). The two measures of income adequacy most often quoted are the U.S. Bureau of Labor Statistics "standard" budgets and the Social Security Administration poverty index. The poverty index is based on the cost of food necessary to provide basic nutritional essentials at the lowest possible cost. The poverty level is three times this cost—adjusted for age, family size, and urban or rural residence. The Bureau of Labor Statistics calculates three budgets (referred to as lower, intermediate, and higher), all of which are adjusted for family size and age. The basic (low) budget is intended to provide for a "modest-but-adequate" level of living rather than the subsistence level reflected in the poverty index. In 1979, the poverty index was about $4200 for a two-person family with the head age 65 or over; the "lower" budget of the Bureau of Labor Statistics was $6023 (U.S. DHHS, 1980b).

Relative Income

Most economic analysts stress the importance of the relative level of income before and after retirement as an indicator of the economic status of the aged. *Replacement ratios* are often used to measure this figure—that is, the ratio of income after retirement to income before retirement. Haanes-Olsen's examination of income replacement rates in selected industrialized nations in 1975 revealed wide variations (see Table 5.1). The majority (75 percent) of the twelve countries provided higher replacement rates for couples than for single retirees. In the United States, Social Security benefits for single workers retiring in 1975 averaged 38 percent of their earnings in the previous year compared with 57 percent for workers with dependent spouses. As shown in Table 5.1, the United States ranked fourth (tied with Canada) in the replacement rate for couples, but eighth in the replacement rate for single retirees. The United Kingdom ranked last among the twelve countries for both categories. Replacement rates shown in Table 5.1 range from 39 percent (United Kingdom) to 76 percent (Sweden) for couples and from 26 percent (United Kingdom) to 67 percent (Italy) for single retirees (Haanes-Olsen, 1978; Atchley, 1980).

Schulz reports that most American couples who retired on Social Security between 1960 and 1980 received less than 40 percent of what their income was before retirement. Even so, this represents a substantial increase over earlier periods. Social Security was never intended to provide for *all* of a retiree's income needs—it was meant

Table 5.1
Earnings Replacement Rates from Public Old-Age Benefits,
Selected Countries, 1975

| Country[a] | Percent of earnings in the year before retirement | |
	Single retiree	Retiree and dependent spouse
Sweden	59	76
Italy	67	67
France	46	65
Canada	39	57
United States	38	57
Norway	41	55
Australia	54	54
Netherlands	38	54
Switzerland	36	53
West Germany	50	50
Denmark	29	43
United Kingdom	26	39

[a]Rank ordered from highest to lowest replacement rates for retiree and dependent spouse.
Source: Adapted from L. Haanes-Olsen, "Earnings Replacement Rate of Old Age Benefits, 1965–75, Selected Countries," Social Security Bulletin 41 (1978): 3–14.

to ensure *some* income that would be supplemented from other sources. Many older persons do have either direct or indirect income from other sources, but over half of their income is from government sources (Schulz, 1980a).

Table 5.2 shows that the proportion of couples and nonmarried individiuals who have income from earnings declines steadily with advancing age. Nearly two-thirds of those age 62 through 64 had earnings income, compared to 45 percent at ages 65 through 67, 35 percent at ages 68 through 69, 27 percent at ages 70 through 72, and only 13 percent at ages 73 and older. The proportion having Social Security income shows a substantial increase between age 64 and 65, followed by a gradual increase with age from 83 percent for the 55 through 67 category to 92 percent for those aged 73 and older. Married couples were more likely than nonmarried persons to have income from earnings and from assets, whereas nonmarried persons were more likely to have income from public assistance programs. These patterns seem to reflect the disadvantaged position of older persons (mainly female), who are widowed, divorced, or never married.

Table 5.2

Income Sources: Percent of Units Aged 55 and Older with Money Income from Specified Sources,[a] by Age and Marital Status, 1978

Source of income	Aged 55–64		Aged 65 and older				
	55–61	62–64	Total	65–67	68–69	70–72	73 and older
Total							
Number (in thousands)	10,066	3,698	18,179	3,806	2,285	3,043	9,045
Percent of units with—							
Earnings	83	66	25	45	35	27	13
Retirement benefits	24	59	93	87	91	94	95
Social Security[b]	14	51	90	83	89	91	92
Benefits other than Social Security	14	27	32	36	34	38	28
Other public pensions	7	11	13	14	13	14	13
Railroad Retirement	c	1	3	2	2	3	3
Government employee pensions	7	10	10	11	11	11	10
Private pensions or annuities	7	16	21	25	23	26	17
Income from assets	61	63	62	62	60	64	61
Interest	57	59	58	59	56	61	58
Other income from assets	23	26	23	23	24	24	23
Veterans' benefits	8	6	5	5	4	4	6
Unemployment compensation	5	3	1	3	1	1	c
Workers' compensation	3	3	1	1	2	1	1
Public assistance	5	6	10	8	10	9	12
Supplemental Security Income	4	5	10	8	9	9	11
Other public assistance	2	1	1	1	2	1	1
Personal contributions	2	c	1	c	1	1	c

(*continued next page*)

71

Table 5.2 (*continued*)
Income Sources: Percent of Units Aged 55 and Older with Money Income from Specified Sources,[a] by Age and Marital Status, 1978

Source of income	Aged 55–64		Total	Aged 65 and older			
	55–61	62–64		65–67	68–69	70–72	73 and older
Married Couples							
Number (in thousands)	6,460	2,183	7,152	1,995	1,011	1,358	2,787
Percent of units with—							
Earnings	93	77	41	59	50	40	26
Retirement benefits	24	57	94	87	92	96	98
Social Security[b]	12	46	91	83	89	93	96
Benefits other than Social Security	15	31	44	45	45	48	40
Other public pensions	9	13	16	16	16	16	16
Railroad Retirement	c	2	3	3	2	3	4
Government employee pensions	8	12	13	13	14	13	12
Private pensions or annuities	7	19	31	33	32	25	27
Income from assets	68	70	71	71	70	74	71
Interest	64	67	68	68	66	70	68
Other income from assets	28	31	29	27	30	31	30
Veterans' benefits	9	7	5	6	3	4	5
Unemployment compensation	6	4	1	3	1	1	1
Workers' compensation	3	3	2	2	2	2	1
Public assistance	2	2	5	4	5	5	6
Supplemental Security Income	1	2	5	3	4	4	6
Other public assistance	1	1	1	1	1	1	1
Personal contributions	1	c	c	c	1	1	c

Nonmarried Persons

Percent of unit with—	3,606	1,515	11,027	181	1,273	1,685	6,257
Number (in thousands)							
Earnings	66	50	15	31	23	17	8
Retirement benefits	24	62	92	88	90	93	94
Social Security[b]	16	58	89	84	88	90	90
Benefits other than Social Security	12	21	25	26	26	30	23
Other public pensions	5	9	12	11	11	13	11
Railroad Retirement	c	1	3	2	2	3	3
Government employee pensions	5	8	9	9	9	10	8
Private pensions or annuities	7	13	14	16	16	18	13
Income from assets	47	53	56	54	52	57	57
Interest	44	48	52	50	43	54	53
Other income from assets	15	20	20	19	20	19	20
Veterans' benefits	7	5	5	4	4	4	6
Unemployment compensation	3	2	1	2	1	1	c
Workers' compensation	2	3	1	1	2	1	1
Public assistance	12	10	14	13	14	13	14
Supplemental Security Income	8	9	13	12	13	12	13
Other public assistance	4	2	2	2	2	2	1
Personal contributions	3	1	1	1	1	1	1

[a]Receipt of sources is ascertained by response to a yes/no question which is imputed by CPS. A married couple receives a source if one or both persons are recipients of that source.

[b]Recipients of Social Security may be receiving retired-worker benefits, dependents' or survivors' benefits, disability benefits, transitionally insured benefits, or special age-72 benefits.

[c]Less than 0.5 percent.

Note: Columns may not add to totals due to rounding.

Source: Social Security Bulletin 44 (1981): 9.

Income Maintenance Programs

Social Security

Initiated in 1935, the United States Social Security program was primarily designed to increase employment opportunities for younger persons. Thus, the old-age retirement benefits were intended to provide some income for the elderly, but also to enable the elderly to leave the labor force in order to make room for younger workers. The 1935 act also provided for the creation of state-administered unemployment compensation programs, to be combined with employment placement services. The act included a "retirement test" for old-age retirement benefits, which is the basis of the limitation on earnings that has become so controversial in recent years (Gray Panthers, 1980; Graebner, 1980; Schulz, 1980a). Since its initiation in 1935, the Social Security program has expanded greatly. The major additions to the program have been survivors' and dependents' benefits in 1939, disability benefits in 1956, and Medicare in 1965. In addition, Social Security coverage was extended to a number of previously ineligible groups, including farm and domestic workers in 1950, self-employed workers in 1954, the uniformed services in 1956, U.S. citizens employed by foreign governments or international organizations in 1960, physicians in 1965, and ministers in 1967. As of 1974, over 90 percent of all Americans age 65 and over were covered under at least one of the Social Security programs, and another 4 percent were covered by other federal retirement plans (Kamerman and Kahn, 1976). The combined Social Security programs are now referred to as OASDHI, which stands for Old Age, Survivors, Disability, and Health Insurance, as opposed to the original OAI (Old Age Insurance) (Snee and Ross, 1978; Hendricks and Hendricks, 1981).

The principles on which Social Security is based are as follows (Schulz, 1980a):

1. Participation is compulsory for members of covered groups. That is, a worker in covered employment does not have the option of being a nonparticipant.
2. Benefits are related to covered earnings.
3. It is intended as one of several potential sources of income maintenance and not as a sole means of support.
4. Funds are to come from special taxes referred to as "contributions."
5. Benefits are weighted to provide higher relative returns for low-income workers, and wages above a cutoff point are not subject to the tax.
6. A person must be retired in order to draw benefits.

Although Social Security is referred to as an insurance program, it is actually a transfer payment program. That is, beneficiaries receive payments from a fund in which current contributions are placed. Thus, the contributions of today's work force are transferred through the fund to those currently receiving benefits. Because of actual and artificial inflation-related increases in benefits, along with changing dependency ratios, both the wage base and the rate of contributions have increased substantially and are expected to increase more in the immediate future.

The intent of the original Social Security program was for contributions to exceed payments so that a substantial reserve fund would accumulate. Two factors have prevented this from happening. First, legislation was amended to provide coverage for previously uncovered groups even though they had paid relatively little into the system. Second, because the reserve fund accumulated and continued rapid growth was predicted based on demographic trends, Congress increased benefits using expected surpluses to pay for the liberalized programs. Because of the expansion of coverage, increases in benefits, inflation, and a decline in the ratio of workers to beneficiaries, the system began to have financial difficulties in the late 1970s. The initial response of government was to increase both the wage base and the contribution ratio for workers' and employers' payroll taxes. For the calendar year 1983, a worker was taxed at the rate of 6.7 percent on earnings through $35,700, or up to $2391.90. This amount was matched by the employers' payroll taxes. Hendricks and Hendricks state that the Social Security payroll tax "has become the largest single tax levied on most independent wage earners" (1981: 285). From 1975 through 1981, Old Age and Survivors Insurance expenditures exceeded receipts, and trust fund reserves reached a dangerously low level. Legislation enacted in 1981 authorized borrowing among the separate Social Security trust funds (Old Age and Survivors Insurance, Disability Insurance, and Medicare) through June, 1983. This legislation also reduced future benefits for certain categories of survivors and dependents. The National Commission on Social Security Reform was appointed in 1982 to analyze the Social Security System and to recommend major legislative action for the mid-1980s (U.S. Senate, 1982).

Additional changes are anticipated in light of predicted demographic trends and financial strains on the system. Interested persons should consult the most recent annual report of the Social Security Board of Trustees for up-to-date information on a changing system.[1] Current information on benefit levels and eligibility may also be obtained from any Social Security office.

[1] See *Annual Report of the Board of Trustees of the Federal Old Age and Survivors Insurance and Disability Trust Funds* (Washington, D.C.: U.S. Government Printing Office).

Supplementary Security Income (SSI)

In 1974, SSI replaced the previous state and federal categorical public assistance programs of old-age assistance, aid to the blind, and aid to the permanently and totally disabled. This program is financed from general revenues and administered through Social Security offices. Basic to the SSI program is a uniform set of eligibility requirements and minimum payment level for all states, although states may add supplements. SSI payments are based on financial need and involve a "means test," with limitations on both income and assets. As of July, 1982, SSI paid up to $284.30 monthly for an individual and $426.40 monthly for an eligible couple. SSI payment levels are adjusted periodically according to changes in the cost of living. The assets test limits nonexcluded assets to $1500 for an individual and to $2250 for a couple. Excluded assets in 1982 were defined as a home, household goods and personal effects worth less than $1500, a car valued at under $1200, and insurance policies with a cash value of under $1500.

Benefits are reduced by 100 percent of unearned income and by 50 percent of earned income above a deductible referred to as the "disregard." In 1982, the disregard was $60 per quarter of unearned income and $85 per month of earned income. Persons eligible for SSI automatically qualify for food stamps, except in a few states in which the food stamp value has been "cashed out" by the supplements to the SSI benefits. Under the food stamp program, participants purchase coupons that are worth more than the purchase price when exchanged for food. However, many eligible older persons fail to participate because of the stigma associated with food stamps (Federal Council on Aging, 1975; U.S. DHHS, 1981).

Private Pensions

The number of workers covered by private pensions has increased substantially since 1940. Schulz estimates that nearly half of the labor force in the United States was covered by a private pension or a deferred profit-sharing plan in 1975. This represents an increase of nearly 400 percent over the proportion having such coverage in 1940 (Schulz, 1980a). The federal government has taken steps to ensure that workers will not lose anticipated benefits from these pension plans. In the past, unemployment, job changes, and company mergers or failures meant that workers could lose all rights to a pension. In 1974, Congress passed the Employee Retirement Income Security Act (ERISA) to protect workers against such loss. This act includes a vesting requirement that assures the workers of at least part of their pensions if they are not still employed by the firm at retirement. The law provides the following three options, one of which must be adopted by employers:

100 percent vesting of benefits after ten years of coverage

25 percent vesting of benefits after five years of service, to be increased by 5 percent for each of the next five years, and by 10 percent for each of the next five years, reaching 100 percent after fifteen years

50 percent vesting when years of service plus employee's age totals 45, and 100 percent vesting five years later, with certain additional conditions concerning years of service.

ERISA also created a branch in the Department of Labor to establish standards for and to monitor pension plans. The act, however, does not require that employers have pension plans, and it has no provision for transfer of pension funds from one employer to another when an employee changes jobs (Atchley, 1980).

Indirect Income

As mentioned earlier, many older people receive indirect income in the form of low-cost or free services, rent subsidies, Medicare and Medicaid, and senior citizen discounts. (Most of these are discussed in this work under the category of the service, such as nutrition, education, housing, or health.) In addition, federal, state, and local taxing authorities provide certain tax breaks for older persons. An example of this type of indirect income is extra exemptions from federal income tax. Some states have similar provisions on state income tax, and practically all states provide for property tax exemptions for older persons. All of these have the effect of adding to available income (Abt Associates, 1975).

Assets

Older persons are more likely than others to have financial assets such as real estate, cash equity in insurance policies, stocks, bonds, and savings accounts. These assets may generate income through interest, dividends, and rents, or they may be liquidated to provide funds, but the value of assets other than home equity is quite low for the majority of the elderly. Atchley reports that most retirees have liquid assets of $2000 or less, exclusive of their homes. Those who have savings often consider them as an emergency fund in case of high medical or other expenses not covered by insurance. They are reluctant to use these funds for daily living costs. Similarly, those who own their homes want to keep them rather than sell them to obtain money for living expenses. After all, they still need a place to live, and having one's own home is highly valued in American society (Atchley, 1980).

Recently, the Federal Home Loan Bank Board has permitted savings and loan associations to offer reverse annuity mortgage (RAM) plans. Under such plans, homeowners can receive a monthly payment from the "reverse mortgage" holder for the rest of their lives or for a specified period. Title to the house then goes to the savings and loan association upon death of the owners or at the end of the period. This arrangement permits individuals to obtain income and yet remain in their homes for the specified period (Schulz, 1980a).

Employment Programs

In response to the interest or need of older persons to be employed, both the public and the private sectors have developed specialized "older worker" programs. The U.S. Department of Labor has operated an older worker program through state employment service offices since the mid-1950s. For purposes of this program, older workers have been identified as those age 45 and over. The basis for using age 45 was strong statistical evidence that persons 45 through 64 had great difficulty obtaining jobs if they became unemployed. In 1967, Congress passed the Age Discrimination in Employment Act, which prohibited discrimination on the basis of age against persons aged 40 through 64. Both the older worker and the age discrimination programs attracted the attention of senior advocacy groups, who pointed out that the legislation implied that it was permissible to discriminate against persons once they had reached age 65. In 1977, the Age Discrimination Act was amended to extend age discrimination protection for nonfederal employees up to age 70 and to eliminate the upper age limit for federal employees. This legislation may or may not increase the proportion of persons who defer retirement, but it does give them a choice (Schulz, 1980a; Lowy, 1979).

Public and private employers have recognized the value of developing "retention" programs for older employees. These often include training components to overcome the "skill obsolescence" that occurs with rapid technological change. (Training for continued employment or for reemployment is discussed in more detail in Chapter 9 of this volume.) Other approaches include job sharing, in which, for example, two employees who want only part-time work may share a full-time position. Some employers provide special assignments to long-term employees as peer counselors, group leaders, and role models for new employees.

Federal Job Programs

The two major federally subsidized job programs for older people are the Senior Community Service Employment Program and the Comprehensive Employment and Training Act (CETA) program. The administration's fiscal year 1983 budget request proposed elimination of these, with establishment of a new special targeted program to replace them and others. These changes were not implemented in fiscal year 1983, and both programs continued under a continuing resolution appropriation. The new program emphasizes training and is directed toward several target groups, including dislocated workers, Indians, farm workers, displaced homemakers, and older workers (U.S. Senate, 1982; U.S. DHHS, 1983).

Title V of the 1978 amendments to the Older Americans Act provides for the Older American Community Service Employment Program. Legislated in 1973 as part of the Older Americans Act, this program was originally administered by the Administration on Aging. In 1975, responsibility for carrying out the program was transferred to the Department of Labor. Until the 1978 amendments, the employment programs were known as Title IX of the act. (The 1978 amendments reorganized the various titles and redesignated the previous Title IX as Title V.) The principal requirement of the legislation was that the Secretary of Labor establish a community service employment program for low-income older persons who wanted to work. Employment can be in public or private nonprofit organizations, in state or local government agencies, or in Indian tribal programs on reservations. The eligible population consists of those persons age 55 or older with low incomes who would have difficulty obtaining employment in the competitive labor market. Program funds are used to pay the workers at minimum wage and to provide physical examinations, appropriate training, and counseling. Goals of the program include skills development, skills renewal, and possible reentry into competitive employment. Agencies in which the workers are placed agree to give full consideration to community service program participants whenever suitable openings occur (U.S. DOL, 1976; NRTA-AARP, 1979). This program has been popular with advocacy groups and with politicians. Although it enjoyed steady growth from its inception through fiscal year 1981, it involves only a small proportion of eligible persons. Most estimates suggest that it provides employment for only about 1 percent of the eligible population (Tenenbaum, 1979; Estes, 1979; Federal Council on the Aging, 1975).

The other major federal employment program that has potential for older persons is provided under the Comprehensive Employment and Training Act (CETA). The purpose of CETA is to provide job training and employment opportunities for economically disadvantaged, unemployed, or underemployed persons, and its goal is to enhance self-sufficiency and to lead to maximum employment. The program is aimed at the "most severely disadvantaged," which includes older workers. Specific activities include assisting in overcoming barriers such as physical impairments and skill obsolescence, paying transportation costs, providing both classroom and on-the-job training, and giving paid work experience. Although CETA is designed for all low-income unemployed persons, in practice it has been directed toward youth. CETA practices vary by state and by local area; some programs do include substantial numbers of older workers. Only about 5 percent of CETA participants nationwide, however, are age 55 or above (Federal Council on the Aging, 1975; Tenenbaum, 1979; Estes, 1979). Estes comments that "the youth oriented Comprehensive Employment and Training Act has done little to meet the needs of older workers" (1979: 94). Tenenbaum's resource book includes a section entitled "CETA—Not for Older People" (1979: 104). Recently interagency agreements have been negotiated between AoA and the Department of Labor calling for increased attention to older workers under CETA programs. However, it is difficult to tell whether or not these agreements have had any significant impact on older-worker opportunities. In addition, CETA is one of the programs targeted for probable elimination in the mid-1980s. Thus its future seems poor, depending on possible political compromises.

Job Bank and Placement Services

Many senior centers and voluntary organizations operate job banks and placement services. The range of positions filled through such services is wide—from intermittent part-time household jobs to full-time permanent positions. Some senior placement services specialize in home repair or housework. They maintain a file of job seekers with particular skills and interests—for example, electrical wiring, plumbing, cooking, or homemaking. In some respects, these programs are similar to those operated for youth through high schools, colleges, and local employment service offices. They are designed for persons who would benefit from temporary, intermittent, or part-time work. Some programs cover the full range of jobs, and still others specialize in business or professional occupations and in second careers for retirees.

Summary

The income level of older persons as a group is substantially lower than that of younger persons. Yet among the older population there is great diversity in the level of income and in assets held. The statistical measures of poverty indices and standard budgets present an overall picture of the aged as an economically deprived group. They appear somewhat better off financially when adjustments are made for indirect income and assets, but a substantial portion of the elderly have total incomes well below the amount needed to maintain the standard of living expected in American society.

The very old are likely to be the most deprived economically. Their retirement income is based on the lower earnings and less liberal benefit programs of an earlier period. These people are likely to have higher expenditures for medical care, drugs, and health-related aids because of the increase in chronic conditions with advanced age. As Schulz points out, though, the very old may not view themselves as being economically deprived because they have lower expectations and have adapted to a less expensive lifestyle.

For many retirees, the only source of direct income is the Social Security system. Expansion of coverage, increased payment levels, and demographic trends have combined to place that system in poor financial condition. After years of substantial benefit increases, the Social Security programs began to cut back in 1981. A number of proposals have been made for overhauling the system: it appears that by the mid-1980s changes in the funding basis and in benefits under the system will be required. The ratio of retirement age to working-age population has changed because of increased life expectancies and declining birth rates, and workers are becoming unwilling or unable to contribute the amounts needed to maintain the system. A partial solution to the income maintenance problem is to encourage older persons to remain in the labor force. This can be done by raising the age at which one becomes eligible for old-age benefits and by providing opportunities and incentives for those already receiving benefits to return to work, either part time or full time.

There is no question that older persons have been discriminated against in hiring and retention policies of many employers, both public and private. There is increasing recognition of the value of older workers and of their need to work for psychological as well as economic reasons. The Social Security program was originally designed to encourage older workers to leave the labor force through the "retirement test." During the 1960s and 1970s, changes in the Social Security system made it possible to retire earlier with reduced benefits, but at the same time the retirement test was relaxed to encourage at least part-time employment. Financial strains on Social Security have led to a number of changes and proposals for changes in the 1980s. One of the proposed changes is a reversal of the trend toward earlier retirement, which would advance the minimum retirement age to a level above 65.

During this same period, federal legislation was enacted making mandatory retirement illegal prior to age 70 and prohibiting discrimination in employment practices on the basis of age. The legislation is difficult to enforce, but seems to have had some impact on employment opportunities for older persons. Employers have initiated programs designed to accommodate some of the problems associated with aging while taking advantage of the many positive attributes of older workers. These programs include retraining, flex time, and job sharing.

The government has attempted to provide opportunities for low-income underemployed or unemployed persons through programs such as Senior Community Service Employment and CETA. Although many older persons in need of work have benefited from these activities, the proportion of the eligible population helped was quite small. Given the demographic, economic, and psychological implications, it seems that opportunities and incentives for continued employment or reemployment for older workers may be expected to increase in the immediate future. It may also be expected that the private sector will assume greater initiative in tapping the potential resource of older workers.

References

Abt Associates, Inc. *Property Tax Relief Programs for the Elderly, Final Report*, prepared for U.S. Department of Housing and Urban Development. Washington, D.C.: U.S. Government Printing Office, 1975.

Atchley, R. C. *The Social Forces in Later Life*, 3rd ed. Belmont, CA: Wadsworth Publishing Co., 1980.

Connell, C. "2-Billion in Social Security Benefit Cuts Largely Unnoticed." *St. Petersburg Times*, August 23, 1981, p. 3A.

Estes, C. L. *The Aging Enterprise*. San Francisco: Jossey-Bass Publishers, 1979.

Federal Council on the Aging. *The Interrelationships of Benefit Programs for the Elderly. Appendix I, Handbook of Federal Programs Benefiting Older Americans*. Washington, D.C.: U.S. Government Printing Office, 1975.

Gray Panthers. *The Gray Panther Manual*, Vol. II. Philadelphia: Gray Panthers, 1980.

Haanes-Olsen, L. "Earnings Replacement Rate of Old Age Benefits, 1965–75, Selected Countries," *Social Security Bulletin* 41 (1978): 3–14.

Hendricks, J., and C. D. Hendricks. *Aging in Mass Society*, 2nd ed. Cambridge, MA: Winthrop Publishers, 1981.

Kamerman, S., and A. Kahn. *Social Services in the United States*. Philadelphia: Temple University Press, 1976.

Lowy, L. *Social Work with the Aged*. New York: Harper and Row Publishers, 1979.

McCoy, J. L., and D. L. Brown. "Health Status among Low-Income Elderly Persons: Rural-Urban Differences." *Social Security Bulletin* 41 (1978): 14–26.

National Retired Teachers Association/American Association of Retired Persons. *Senior Community Service Employment Programs*. Washington, D.C.: NRTA-AARP, 1979.

Schulz, J. *The Economics of Aging*, 2nd ed. Belmont, CA: Wadsworth Publishing Co., 1980a.

_____. "Social Security's Future." *Generations*: 4, 1 (May, 1980b): 21–23.

Sheppard, H. L., and S. E. Rix. *The Graying of Working America: The Coming Crisis of Retirement Age Policy*. New York: The Free Press, 1977.

Snee, J., and M. Ross. "Social Security Amendments of 1977: Legislative History and Summary of Provisions." *Social Security Bulletin* 41 (1978): 3–20.

Tenenbaum, F. *Over 55 Is Not Illegal*. Boston, MA: Houghton Mifflin Co., 1979.

U.S. Bureau of the Census. *Social and Economic Characteristics of the Older Population: 78*, Current Population Reports, Series P-23, No. 85. Washington, D.C.: U.S. Government Printing Office, 1979.

U.S. Department of Health, Education and Welfare, National Center for Health Statistics. *Current Estimates from the National Health Survey, United States, 1976*, DHEW Pub. No. (PHS) 78-1547. Hyattsville, MD: NCHS, 1977a.

_____, Administration on Aging. "Income and Poverty among the Elderly: 1975." In *Statistical Reports on Older Americans No. 2*, DHEW Pub. No. (OHDS) 77-20286. Washington, D.C.: U.S. Government Printing Office, 1977b.

_____, Administration on Aging. *Facts About Older Americans, 1979*, DHHS Pub. No. (PHS) 80-20006. Washington, D.C.: U.S. Government Printing Office, 1980a.

_____, Administration on Aging. "The Older Worker." In *Statistical Reports on Older Americans No. 6*, DHHS Pub. No. (OHDS) 81-20265. Washington, D.C.: U.S. Government Printing Office, 1980b.

_____, Social Security Administration. *SSI for the Aged, Blind, and Disabled*. Washington, D.C.: U.S. Government Printing Office, 1981.

_____. "Report on Activities in Aging: A Report to the House Committee on Appropriations." Washington, D.C.: Administration on Aging, January, 1983 (unpublished).

U.S. Department of Labor. "Senior Community Service Employment

Program Rules and Regulations." *Federal Register*, Vol. 41, 1976, pp. 9066–9082.

U.S. House of Representatives, Select Committee on Aging. *Welfare Reform and the Elderly Poor (Part I)*. Washington, D.C.: U.S. Government Printing Office, 1977.

U.S. Senate, Special Committee on Aging. *Future Directions in Social Security, Part 19*. Washington, D.C.: U.S. Government Printing Office, 1976.

_____, Special Committee on Aging. *The Proposed Fiscal Year 1983 Budget: What It Means for Older Americans*. Washington, D.C.: U.S. Government Printing Office, 1982.

White House Conference on Aging. *Delegate Work Book on Income*. Washington, D.C.: White House Conference on Aging, 1971a.

_____. *Employment: Background and Issues*. Washington, D.C.: 1971 White House Conference on Aging, 1971b.

_____. *Income: Background and Issues*. Washington, D.C.: 1971 White House Conference on Aging, 1971c.

_____. *Retirement: Background and Issues*. Washington, D.C.: 1971 White House Conference on Aging, 1971d.

_____. *Toward a National Policy on Aging: Proceedings of the 1971 White House Conference on Aging*, Vols. I and II. Washington, D.C.: U.S. Government Printing Office, 1973.

Chapter

6

Health Status and Health Services

The World Health Organization (WHO) defines health as "a state of complete physical, mental, and social well being and not just the absence of disease or infirmity" (White House Conference on Aging, 1971; Albrecht and Higgins, 1979; Wolinsky, 1980). This definition attempts to emphasize the positive side of health and the interrelationship among physical, psychological, and social factors. So defined, however, health is difficult if not impossible to measure. Positive health is both relative and subjective. What is considered to be good health for one individual or group may not be thought of as good for another individual or group. Because of these conceptual problems in measuring positive health, most analyses continue to concentrate on measures of nonhealth. "Good health," then, is defined in terms of relative freedom from diseases, symptoms, mental or emotional problems, and impairments. Relatively high rates of these conditions are considered to reflect poor health. Measurement of health status of a population is usually based on death rates and causes of death, extent and nature of acute and chronic conditions, sensory defects, and rates of impairments of activity and mobility (U.S. DHEW, 1977b).

The presence of morbid conditions (departures from health) in a population suggests a need for some type of intervention, which may be curative or preventive in either the primary or the secondary sense. As the term implies, *curative intervention* has the goal of eliminating a morbid condition that already exists. *Primary prevention* attempts to keep people from acquiring a morbid condition, whereas *secondary prevention* limits the progress of the condition or reduces the extent of associated impairment.

Chronic and Infectious Diseases

Except for immunization, sanitation, and insect and rodent control programs (largely the area of public health), the major focus of medicine in the United States has been curative and restorative rather than preventive. The development of antibiotics and other drugs contributed greatly to the control of infectious diseases, which were the leading cause of death in the early 1900s. There is increasing recognition, however, that the techniques used to deal with infectious diseases may not be appropriate for the prevention and treatment of chronic illnesses.

By definition, chronic diseases are of long duration. The cause is often unknown, although certain social, psychological, behavioral, and environmental conditions have been found to be associated with certain chronic diseases. The course of the disease is usually progressive and irreversible. The objectives of treatment are control of symptoms, maintenance, and rehabilitation. Primary and secondary prevention may involve modification of the patient's lifestyle through changes in work patterns, environment, eating and drinking habits, or ways of dealing with stress.

Infectious diseases, on the other hand, are usually reversible, self-limiting, of short duration, and caused by a known organism. Treatment is directed toward the causal organism, and the goal is cure (Kart et al., 1978).

Health Care Costs

Modern medicine has made great advances in technology, especially since World War II. New drugs, organ transplants, life-support systems, and sophisticated diagnostic procedures are among the achievements that have improved health care. Requirements for equipment, facilities, and specialized training, though, have resulted in rapidly increasing care costs.

Between 1965 and 1977, expenditures for health care more than quadrupled, increasing from just under $39 billion to over $162 billion. At the same time, the proportion of the U.S. gross national product spent on health care increased from 5.9 percent to 8.8 percent (U.S. Senate, 1979). The Department of Health, Education and Welfare estimates that about half of the dollar increase was related to higher costs of goods and services; another 40 percent to the increased complexity of care, quality improvements, and increased utilization; and the remaining 10 percent to population growth (U.S. DHEW, 1977b.) Many people, particularly the elderly, would be unable to afford these costs without some form of financial assistance, such as that provided by Medicare and Medicaid.

Approaches to Treatment

Medical Model

Traditional health care in the United States follows the medical model. In this model, illness is considered to be organically based, involuntary, socially unacceptable, and treatable only by physicians (Albrecht and Higgins, 1979). Critics of this model refer to health care in the United States as "sickness care," oriented toward medical intervention for those defined as sick rather than toward prevention of illness and promotion of social and psychological well-being (Kuhn et al., 1980). Critics are particularly dissatisfied with the approach of the medical model to the chronic and degenerative diseases often associated with aging (Albrecht and Higgins, 1979).

Holistic Health

Dissatisfaction with the medical model has spurred interest in the holistic model. The holistic approach focuses on the "whole person" within his or her social, psychological, and physical environments. The emphasis is on prevention and natural healing. Kuhn describes the holistic concept as one that brings together "physical, mental, spiritual, and environmental health, recognizing (1) the human body's healing capacity, and (2) the interaction between economic and social conditions of society and the health and well-being of the people" (Gray Panthers, 1980: III-14-1). Promoters of the new holistic movement stress alternatives to medical treatment such as biofeedback, diet therapy, acupuncture, relaxation, and meditation (Gray Panthers, 1980).

Family Practice Medicine

A relatively new "specialty" is family practice. Actually, the concepts of family practice and specialty seem to be contradictory, since the family practice physician specializes in being a generalist. That is, this physician follows the whole-person approach and provides diagnosis and treatment within the context of the patient's social environment. The seven characteristics identified by Webber as distinguishing family practice physicians are (1) they are the first contact of the patient with the treatment system, (2) they are readily accessible, (3) they are knowledgeable about and coordinate all aspects of health care, (4) they are the source of a major portion of the patient's care, (5) they ensure continuity of care, (6) they treat the patient within a social context, and (7) they are oriented toward the whole patient (Webber, 1976). In order to carry out these functions, these physicians need considerable training in the social and behavioral sciences. Family practice incorporates elements of both traditional medicine and the holistic approach and seems to represent a movement toward a broader concept of health.

Health Status of Older Persons

The most extreme measure of departure from health is *mortality*. Mortality measures, such as total (crude) death rate, causes of death, and average life expectancy, are often used as indicators of a population's health status. Data on mortality are reported periodically by the U.S. National Center for Health Statistics and by state vital statistics units. Other measures, which focus on the living, include incidence and prevalence of acute and chronic conditions, measures of impairment or disability, and self-reported health status (U.S. DHEW, 1977b; Hickey, 1980; Hendricks and Hendricks, 1981). Perhaps the most comprehensive source of data on morbidity is the National Center for Health Statistics, which conducts continuing surveys of the general population and health care providers and reports on illness, injuries, disability, use of resources, and other topics (U.S. DHHS, 1981b; U.S. DHEW, 1977a).

Mortality and Expectation of Life

The total death rate in the United States declined from 14.7 per thousand population (all ages) in 1910 to 8.8 per thousand population in 1978. During the same period, the average expectation of life from birth increased from about 50 years to over 73 years. As mentioned before, much of this increase resulted from reductions in infant and childhood mortality. The infant mortality rate (deaths of infants under 1 year of age per thousand live births during a given year) dropped from nearly a hundred (estimated) in 1910 to around ten in 1978 (Smith and Zopf, 1970; U.S. DHEW, 1979). Thus, the infant born in 1978 had a far greater chance of surviving to adulthood and old age. In 1900, the three leading causes of death were influenza/ pneumonia, tuberculosis, and gastroenteritis, generally classified as infectious diseases. The leading causes in 1978 were heart disease, cancer, and cerebral vascular disease, generally classified as chronic diseases (Albrecht and Higgings 1979; Hendricks and Hendricks, 1981).

Chronic Conditions

Rates of chronic conditions increase directly with advancing age. The National Health Survey reports that about 85 percent of the noninstitutionalized older persons have one or more chronic conditions (U.S. DHEW, 1979). The most common conditions are arthritis, hypertension, and heart disease (U.S. DHEW, 1977a). Of these, hypertension and heart disease are major contributors to death as well as to disability. Arthritis, on the other hand, seldom causes death, but it is a major cause of limitations of activity and mobility. In 1975, about 47 percent of older people not in institutions had some limitation of activity because of chronic conditions. Approximately 40 percent were limited in major activity, defined as working or keeping house. Heart disease accounted for 24 percent of the cases, and arthritis/rheumatism accounted for an additional 23 percent (U.S. DHEW, 1977a). Data on limitations of mobility (inability to move about freely) for the year 1972 show that about one-fifth of the elderly had some limitation. Altogether, 5 percent were homebound, and an additional 7 percent required help in getting around (U.S. DHEW, 1977a; U.S. DHHS, 1980a). Significant impairment of hearing affects nearly 30 percent of older persons, and about 20 percent of the elderly report visual impairments severe enough to limit some activities (U.S. Senate, 1979).

Self-Rating of Health

Although most older persons have at least one chronic condition and a high proportion are limited in activity, few consider themselves to be in poor health. In response to the self-rating question in the National Health Survey, over two-thirds of those age 65 and above rated their health as good or excellent and less than one-tenth assessed their health as being poor (U.S. DHEW, 1977b). This suggests that the complete absence of morbid conditions is not a prerequisite to subjectively classified good health. Even though chronic conditions may cause some interference with physical and social functioning, most older persons find that such interference is not severe enough to cause them to think of themselves as being in poor health.

Use of Traditional Health Services

"Traditional" health services are those basic to the medical model: physician visits, clinic services, nursing home care, and hospital treatment. Reasonably accurate estimates of utilization rates for the basic health resources are compiled and reported periodically by the National Center for Health Statistics (U.S. DHEW, 1979; U.S. DHHS, 1980b). In some data, services are reported by type of setting. The three broad categories of settings used by the National Center are ambulatory care, in-patient care, and home care. Figure 6.1 outlines health resources by the type of facility and by setting. Although reports are published on all types of resources, only selected categories are reported for the population age 65 and over. Figure 6.2, prepared by the Federal Council on Aging, shows projections of the use of selected health resources by older persons for the year 2000.

Use of Physicians

In 1978, persons age 65 plus who were not in institutions averaged 6.3 physician contacts per year. Most of these were visits to the physician's office (73.4 percent), but the 6.3 average includes contact with doctors in hospitals, in out-patient clinics, in other clinics, and by telephone (less than one-tenth of the contacts were made by telephone). At the time of the National Health Survey interview, four-fifths of all older persons had used a physician's services within the past year.

Use of Short-Stay Hospitals

Hospital use is reported in terms of discharges per thousand noninstitutionalized persons and in terms of average length of stay. Predictably, older persons had much higher rates of hospitalization than younger persons in 1978 and stayed longer in the facility when hospitalized. For every thousand noninstitutionalized elderly, there were 412 discharges from nonfederal short-stay hospitals, compared with 154 per thousand population of all ages. The average length of stay for older persons was 11 days, compared with about 7 days for younger persons. Total expenditures for short-stay hospital care were estimated at $85.3 billion in 1979, representing about 40 percent of all health care expenditures (U.S. DHHS, 1980b).

Use of Nursing Homes

Table 6.1 summarizes rates of residency in nursing homes by age categories for selected years. Between 1973 and 1977, the percentage of all older persons who were in nursing homes increased from 3.7 percent to 4.8 percent. For all years, there was a substantially higher rate of nursing home residence for the very old (age 85 and over) than for the relatively young old (ages 65 through 74). The rate of nursing home use for the group aged 65 to 74 increased from 1.16 percent in 1969 to 1.23 percent in 1974 and to 1.45 percent in 1977. A similar pattern is shown for the group aged 75 to 84, but not for the group aged 85 and over, for whom use increased between 1969 and 1974, then decreased between 1974 and 1977 (U.S. DHHS, 1980b; U.S. DHEW, 1979). Since most nursing home care is paid for by public funds, the changing rates in use of facilities over time by age may be partially related to changes in public policy. For example, both the deinstitutionalization and the continuum-of-care policies described earlier in this volume probably had some impact on nursing home utilization patterns.

Health Care Financing

Total health care expenditures in the United States were estimated at $212.2 billion in 1979 (U.S. DHHS, 1980b). The older population (65 and over) accounted for about 30 percent of this amount, or roughly $63.7 billion (U.S. DHHS, 1980a, b). Per capita costs for older persons were estimated at $1745 in 1977, nearly three and one-half times that of persons under the age of 65 ($514) (U.S. Senate, 1979).[1] The higher health care expenses of older persons are, of course, directly related to their higher rates of chronic conditions

[1]There appears to be a discrepancy between the 30 percent of total expenditure figure from DHHS and the 340 percent (nearly three and one-half times) per capita figure reported by the U.S. Senate. This probably reflects the use of different dates and different data sources.

Figure 6.1   Health Care Resources by Setting and by Type of Facility or Care

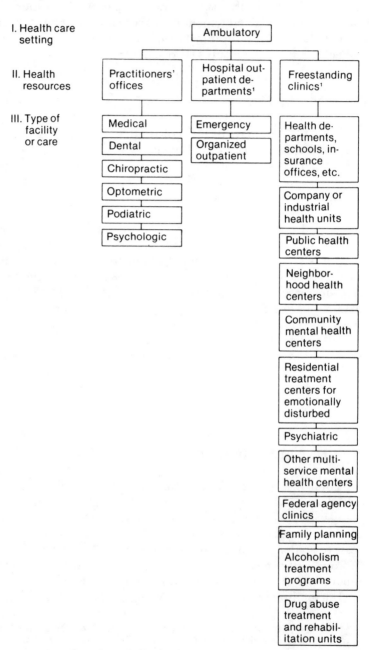

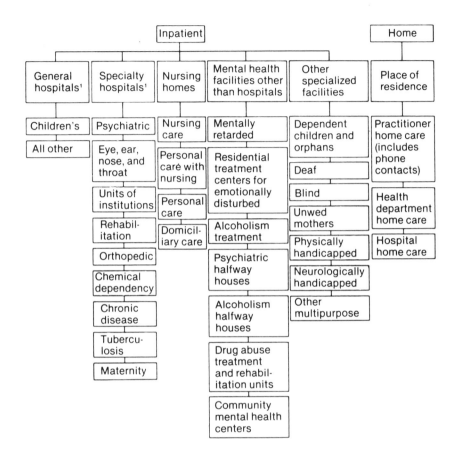

[1]Facilities of specific federal agencies are individually distinguished in various chapters of this report.

Source: U.S. Department of Health, Education and Welfare, National Center for Health Statistics, *The Nation's Use of Health Resources: 1979*, DHEW Pub. No. (PHS) 80-1240 (Hyattsville, MD: NCHS, 1979), p. 6.

Figure 6.2   Projections of the Use of Health Services by the Elderly: United States, 1978 and 2000

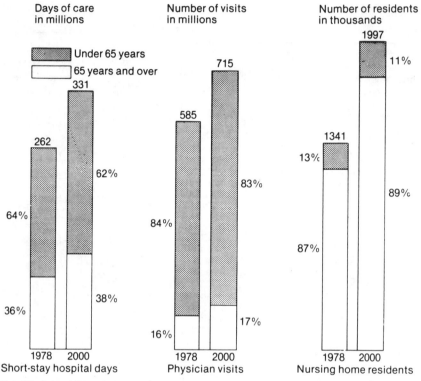

Note: Physician visits exclude telephone contacts and visits to clinics and emergency rooms.

Source: U.S. Department of Health and Human Services, Federal Council on Aging, *The Need for Long Term Care* (Washington, D.C.: U.S. Government Printing Office, 1981), p. 55.

Table 6.1
Residence in Nursing Homes by Age Category for Selected Years, U.S. Population Age 65 and Over (rate per 1,000 population)

	1977	1974	1969
Ages 65 and over	47.9	45.1	37.1
Ages 65–74	14.5	12.3	11.6
Ages 75–84	68.0	59.4	51.7
Ages 85 +	216.4	253.7	203.2

Source: U.S. Department of Health and Human Services, *Health, United States: 1980*, DHHS Pub. No. (PHS) 81-1232 (Hyattsville, MD: NCHS, 1980).

and associated greater use of hospitals, nursing homes, physicians' services, and other resources. Figures from a U.S. Senate Special Committee report show that 44 percent of money spent on health care for older persons went for hospital care, 26 percent for nursing home care, 17 percent for physician services, and 7 percent for drugs. About two-thirds of all health expenditures for the elderly are provided through public funds (U.S. DHHS, 1980a; U.S. Senate, 1979). In 1977, 44.3 percent came from Medicare, 16.7 percent from Medicaid, and 6 percent from several smaller programs, including that of the Veterans Administration (U.S. Senate, 1979).

Table 6.2 and Figure 6.3 summarize the sources of payment on a per capita basis by age category. For older persons, payments by individuals (out of pocket) increased from $237 per person in 1966 to $463 per person in 1977. During the same period, the percentage of total costs paid by individuals as opposed to third-party payers decreased from 53.2 percent to 31.9 percent and the percentage of total costs paid by government increased from 29.8 percent to 67.0 percent.

Medicare

Medicare is a federal health insurance program that was legislated in 1965 as Title XVIII of the Social Security Act. There are two parts to the Medicare program: Part A, which covers basic hospitalization and certain post-hospitalization costs, and Part B, which covers physician services and out-patient therapy under specified conditions. Part A coverage is automatic for any person qualified for Social Security or a railroad pension either as an insured worker or as an eligible survivor or dependent of an insured worker. Persons who attained age 65 before 1968 but had insufficient coverage for retirement benefits are also covered by Medicare. Older persons not eligible on the basis of the above requirements may buy Part A coverage by paying a monthly premium, which is adjusted periodically. For the year beginning July 1, 1982, the Part A premium was $113 per month. Part B of Medicare is optional and requires payment of a monthly fee that is adjusted periodically. For the year beginning July 1, 1982, the Part B premium was $12.20 per month. Current rates for Part A and Part B may be obtained from any local Social Security office.

Part A of Medicare is financed by a portion of the Social Security payroll tax that finances old-age and disability retirement programs. As of 1980, the contribution rate for Part A was 1.05 percent of earnings covered by Social Security and was included in the 6.65 percent Social Security tax. Part B is financed by the monthly

Table 6.2
Per Capita Medical Care Expenditures by Age Group and by Source of Payment, 1966 and 1977

Age and year	Total	Direct out-of-pocket	Third-party payments			
			Total	Government	Private health insurance	Philanthropy and industry
Amount:						
under 65:						
1966	$ 155	$ 79	$ 76	$ 30	$ 42	$ 3
1977	514	164	350	150	187	13
65 plus:						
1966	445	237	209	133	71	5
1977	1745	463	1282	1169	101	13
Distribution (percent):						
under 65:						
1966	100.0	51.1	48.9	19.4	27.3	2.2
1977	100.0	31.9	68.1	29.1	36.4	2.6
65 plus:						
1966	100.0	53.2	46.8	29.8	15.9	1.0
1977	100.0	26.5	73.5	67.0	5.8	0.0

Source: U.S. Senate, Special Committee on Aging, *Developments in Aging: 1978, Part I* (Washington, D.C.: U.S. Government Printing Office, 1979), p. XX.

Figure 6.3   Per Capita Health Care Expenditures for the Elderly by Type of Care and Source of Payment: United States, 1978

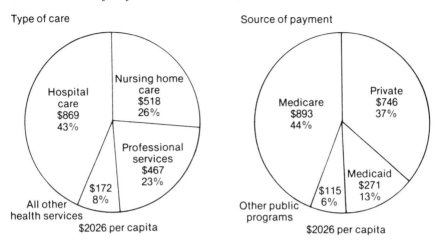

Note: Other health services include drugs and drug sundries, eyeglasses and appliances, and other health services.

Source: U.S. Department of Health and Human Services, Federal Council on Aging, *The Need for Long Term Care* (Washington, D.C.: U.S. Government Printing Office, 1981), p. 51.

premium payments plus appropriations of federal general revenue funds. Over nine-tenths of all persons age 65 and above are covered by Medicare health insurance (U.S. DHEW, 1980a; Federal Council on the Aging, 1975).

The Medicare program provides only partial payment for covered services, and the services covered are restricted. The focus is on curative and rehabilitative care; both preventive and long-term supportive care are specifically excluded from coverage. Overall, Medicare pays for less than half of the medical expenses of older Americans (U.S. Senate, 1979; Hendricks and Hendricks, 1981; Gray Panthers, 1980). As of 1983, Medicare Part A paid for all basic hospital expenses except the first $304 (the deductible) for up to 60 days of hospitalization. From the sixty-first through the ninetieth day of hospitalization, Part A paid for all except $76 per day of basic hospital charges. The $76 per day, which was paid by the patient or some other party on the patient's behalf, is referred to as "coinsurance." Extended care facility (nursing home) payment is covered under Part A only when prescribed by the attending physician following a period of hospitalization of at least three days. Coinsurance for extended care begins after the twentieth day at a rate of $38.50 per day (1983) for up to 80 more days (U.S. DHHS, 1983b).

Part B of Medicare pays 80 percent of "reasonable charges" for covered services, including doctors' fees, drugs or supplies provided by a doctor, emergency room fees, prescribed therapy, equipment, and so on, after a deductible has been met. Because of the way in which the term "reasonable charges" is defined, many older persons find that Part B pays less than 80 percent of the covered expense. That is, physician charges often exceed the amount defined as reasonable, and the patient is responsible for paying the difference. The Gray Panthers report that the average Part B patient pays about 40 percent of actual charges in the San Francisco Bay area. The relationship between "reasonable" and actual charges varies from one geographic area to another and from one physician to another within the same area (Gray Panthers, 1980). A Social Security Administration pamphlet on Medicare states, "Because of the way reasonable charges are determined under the law, they may be lower than the actual charges made by doctors and suppliers" (U.S. DHEW, 1980a: 12). "Reasonable charges" are based on the lesser of the treating physician's customary charge for the service in at least half of his or her billings during the base year or the amount charged at least three-fourths of the time by other physicians in the same geographic area. The base year is updated each July for the previous complete calendar year. Part B does not cover preventive services, hearing aids, dental care, prescription drugs, and many other services.

Medicaid

The Medical Assistance Program provided for under Title XIX of the Social Security Act is commonly referred to as Medicaid. This is a joint federal-state program designed to provide health care for the poor, regardless of age. The eligibility requirements and the services covered by Medicaid vary from state to state, and the federal share of funding is determined by a formula that provides a higher ratio of federal-to-state funds for poorer states. The federal share ranges from 50 percent to 83 percent of health care payments under the state program, depending on the state's per capita income and the nature of coverage under the state Medicaid plan. Although the federal regulations set minimum standards regarding the nature of the "means test" and the types of services offered, there are wide variations among the states. Medicaid can pay for prescription drugs, eyeglasses, supportive services, and long-term nursing home care in addition to the basic medical treatment services covered by Medicare. Although Medicaid is a welfare-type program based on restrictive limitations of income and assets, it is a major source of payment for long-term care (mainly in nursing homes) (U.S. DHEW, 1980b; Federal Council on Aging, 1975; Estes, 1979). The Administration on

Aging reports that Medicaid paid almost $7.2 billion for health care for older persons in fiscal year 1983 (U.S. DHHS, 1983a).

Summary

Health status is usually defined and measured in a negative sense. That is, various indicators of nonhealth or sickness are the basis for labeling persons as being in relatively good or relatively poor health. Old age is generally associated with declining health, as reflected by high rates of chronic conditions, sensory losses, and limitations of activity and mobility. Yet the majority of older persons rate them-selves as being in good or excellent health as compared with others their age and are able to maintain fairly active lifestyles. The traditional model for health care in the United States is the medical model, which focuses on cure and rehabilitation rather than pre-vention. Critics suggest that this may not be the best approach to health care, particularly in dealing with the chronic and degenerative diseases associated with aging, and they offer a number of alternatives with a more holistic orientation and with much greater emphasis on prevention than on cure.

The costs of health care for the elderly have been increasing rapidly because of inflation, greater utilization, and more complex treatment resources. The major federal programs that assist in payment for health care are Medicare and Medicaid, which together paid for an estimated three-fifths (61 percent) of all health care for older persons in 1977.

References

Albrecht, G. L., and P. C. Higgins, eds. *Health, Illness, and Medicine.* Chicago: Rand McNally College Publishing Co., 1979.

Estes, C. L. *The Aging Enterprise.* San Francisco: Jossey-Bass Publishers, 1979.

Federal Council on the Aging. *The Interrelationships of Benefit Programs for the Elderly. Appendix I, Handbook of Federal Programs Benefiting Older Americans.* Washington, D.C.: U.S. Government Printing Office, 1975.

Graebner, W. *A History of Retirement.* New Haven, CT: Yale University Press, 1980.

Gray Panthers. *The Gray Panther Manual,* Vol. II. Philadelphia: Gray Panthers, 1980.

Hendricks, J., and C. D. Hendricks. *Aging in Mass Society*, 2nd ed. Cambridge, MA: Winthrop Publishers, 1981.

Hickey, T. *Health and Aging*. Monterey, CA: Brooks/Cole Publishing Co., 1980.

Kart, C. S., E. S. Metress, and J. F. Metress. *Aging and Health: Biologic and Social Perspectives*. Menlo Park, CA: Addison-Wesley Publishing Co., 1978.

Kuhn, M., R. Skeist, and J. Grottenthaler. "Holistic Health." In *The Gray Panther Manual*, Vol. II, pp. III-14-1, 2. Philadelphia: Gray Panthers, 1980.

Lawton, A. H. "Clinical Gerontology Is Social Medicine." In *Total Health and Aging*, eds. W. C. Martin and A. J. E. Wilson III, pp. 123–134. St. Petersburg, FL: Eckerd College Gerontology Center, 1976.

Smith, T. L., and P. E. Zopf. *Demography: Principles and Methods*. Philadelphia: F. A. Davis Co., 1970.

U.S. Department of Health and Human Services, Administration on Aging. *Facts about Older Americans, 1979*, DHHS Pub. No. (PHS) 80-20006. Washington, D.C.: U.S. Government Printing Office, 1980a.

_____, Health Resources Administration. *Health, United States: 1980*, DHHS Pub. No. (PHS) 81-1232. Hyattsville, MD: NCHS, 1980b.

_____, Administration on Aging. "Older Americans Month May, 1981, Information Package." Washington, D.C.: AoA, 1981a.

_____, National Center for Health Statistics. *Prevalence of Selected Impairments, U.S. 1977*, Series 10, No. 134. Hyattsville, MD: NCHS, 1981b.

_____. "Report on Activities in Aging: A Report to the House Committee on Appropriations." Washington, D.C.: Administration on Aging, January, 1983a (unpublished).

_____, Social Security Administration. *A Brief Explanation of Medicare*. Washington, D.C.: U.S. Government Printing Office, 1983b.

U.S. Department of Health, Education and Welfare, National Center for Health Statistics. *Current Estimates from the Health Interview Survey*, Series 10, No. 126. Hyattsville, MD: NCHS, 1977a.

_____, Health Resources Administration. *Health, United States: 1976–77*. Washington, D.C.: U.S. Government Printing Office, 1977b.

_____, National Center for Health Statistics. *The Nation's Use of Health Resources: 1979*, DHEW Pub. No. (PHS) 80-1240. Hyattsville, MD: NCHS, 1979.

_____, Social Security Administration. *A Brief Explanation of Medicare*. Washington, D.C.: U.S. Government Printing Office, 1980a.

_____, National Center for Health Statistics. "Provisional Statistics Annual Summary for the U.S., 1979." *Monthly Vital Statistics Report*. Hyattsville, MD: NCHS, 1980b.

U.S. Senate, Special Committee on Aging. *Developments in Aging: 1978, Part I*. Washington, D.C.: U.S. Government Printing Office, 1979.

Webber, I. L. "The Social Sciences and Quality of Care." In *Total Health and Aging*, eds. W. C. Martin and A. J. E. Wilson III, pp. 29–42. St. Petersburg, FL: Eckerd College Gerontology Center, 1976.

White House Conference on Aging. *Physical and Mental Health: Background and Issues*. Washington, D.C.: White House Conference on Aging, 1971.

Wolinsky, F. D. *The Sociology of Health*. Boston: Little, Brown and Co., 1980.

Chapter

7

Housing Services

Living arrangements affect the degree of independence, security, accessibility of services, privacy, and social involvement of persons of all ages. Housing type, quality, and location become increasingly important with advancing age, especially for those who have some degree of functional limitation or transportation problems (Montgomery, 1972; Bylund et al., 1980; Lawton, 1980; Atchley, 1980). The need for variety in housing for the elderly is generally recognized. Needs vary by lifestyle, economic situation, health, family composition and relationships, need for supportive services, and personal preferences.

Housing Policies

One of the objectives of the Older Americans Act is to assure opportunities for "suitable housing, independently selected, designed and located with reference to special needs and available at costs which older citizens can afford" (U.S. DHEW, 1979: 2). Housing was a major policy issue at the three White House Conferences on Aging in 1961, 1971, and 1981. The background paper on housing for the 1971 conference summarized the concerns expressed in connection with these conferences: "[the nature of housing] may determine whether they can live independently or in an institution; a solitary or a social life; in safety or in danger; or in extreme cases, whether they live or die" (White House Conference on Aging, 1971: 1). The final report of the 1971 White House Conference suggested that a national policy on housing must provide a choice for older persons and should include development of new and rehabilitated units produced by the public, private nonprofit, and private profit sectors. This report recommended production of at least 120,000 new units annually; government funding at the federal, state, and local levels; a range of facilities to meet different and changing needs relative to support services and home maintenance; and specialized programs for rural and minority aged (White House Conference on Aging, 1973).

The 1981 White House Conference on Aging reaffirmed the 1949 Housing Act goal calling for suitable housing for all elderly persons and recommended that "no fewer than 200,000 units for the elderly should be provided within all levels of government and the private sector" (White House Conference on Aging, 1981: 87). In commenting on the 1971 recommendation for 120,000 new units per year, Lawton said, "This goal has been missed by a mile, and with the increasing tightness of money, the goal is less and less realistic" (1980: 100). The fiscal year 1983 federal budget request seems to indicate that Lawton's evaluation of the situation was correct. The Senate Special Committee on Aging estimated that reductions in federal housing support for low-income elderly persons in 1983 would total $428 million (U.S. Senate, 1982).

Housing location and type affect the accessibility of such services as electricity, telephone, water, and transportation as well as the availability and efficiency of the full range of informal and formal community supports. Many of the problems associated with old age could be reduced or eliminated through improvements in living arrangements (White House Conference on Aging, 1973).

The diversity of physical, mental, and social needs of the elderly is the basis for a suggested "continuum of housing types." This continuum would range from totally independent residences to total-care institutions. Between the extremes would be residential arrangements linked to supportive services (Tibbitts, 1977; Benedict, 1979; Atchley, 1980). This concept follows the rationale of the least restrictive environment and of the coordinated continuum of care, described in Chapter 2.

Characteristics of Older Persons' Housing

Data from the Bureau of the Census show that in 1975 older persons (65 plus) made up about one-tenth of the total U.S.

population but about one-fifth of all household heads. Between 1970 and 1975, there was an 11 percent increase in the number of older persons and a 16 percent increase in the number of households headed by them. Older persons residing in nonmetropolitan areas were more likely to own their homes than were their metropolitan counterparts (83 percent compared with 65 percent). The 1975 data showed that residences of older persons were generally older than those of younger persons—nearly half of the residences of the elderly were built prior to 1940 and only 10 percent were built after 1970. (About one-third of all U.S. housing units were built before 1940, and 15 percent were built after 1970.) Although the relationship is not absolute, older homes usually need more extensive maintenance and repair and are more likely to be deficient in terms of plumbing and kitchen facilities. Nearly two-thirds of older persons lived in detached single dwellings as opposed to multi-unit buildings.

A small but increasing proportion of the elderly lived in mobile homes (Bylund et al., 1980; Lawton, 1980). Lawton reports that the proportion of older persons residing in mobile homes was 4.9 percent in 1976 (based on census data) but that this figure reflected an increase of 23 percent between 1973 and 1976 (Lawton, 1980). Older persons were overrepresented among mobile-home dwellers, and most of them (92 percent) owned their homes as opposed to renting them. Nearly half of these homes were located either by themselves on single plots of ground or in groupings of five or less. Those located in areas of higher concentration (usually in mobile home parks) were more likely to have public water and sewage facilities and better access to police and fire protection, health and social services, and shopping (Lawton, 1980).

Design Factors

Features may be designed into new and remodeled housing to help maintain the elderly's independence and to enhance the quality of life of older persons. Projects intended for the aged and the physically impaired incorporate features such as ramps in place of steps, levers instead of doorknobs, and support rails in bathrooms. Environmental design may also ease social interaction and increase access to home-delivered and community support services (Wilson, 1971; White House Conference on Aging, 1973; Lawton, 1980). Such plans are of extreme importance in maintaining frail or vulnerable older persons (Atchley, 1980). Investments of time and money to develop positive aspects of environment are often repaid over the life of a building through increased use and efficiency.

Table 7.1
U.S. Department of Housing and Urban Development Programs
That Have Been Used for Housing for the Elderly

Type of program	Sponsor			
	Nonprofit	For-profit	Limited dividend	Other
Mortgage Insurance				
221(d)(3): rental or cooperative	yes	no	yes	public
221(d)(4): rental or cooperative	no	yes	no	no
231: housing for the elderly	yes	yes	yes	public
213: cooperatives	yes	no	no	yes
Direct Loan				
202: housing for the elderly and handicapped	yes	no	no	no
106(b): seed money loans (related to 202)	yes	no	no	no
Rental Assistance:				
8: lower-income rent assistance	yes	yes	yes	yes

Source: Prepared by Priscilla Murray, International Center for Social Gerontology, under Grant #90-A-1214, Administration on Aging, 1979.

Housing Programs

The four major types of housing programs provided through agencies are maintenance and repair, rent supplements, government-guaranteed loans for construction (mortgage insurance), and direct government loans for construction (see Table 7.1). Other programs include congregate and shared housing; specialized housing programs may be sponsored by private enterprises, nonprofit organizations, or public agencies. The major federal housing programs are administered by the Department of Housing and Urban Development (HUD) and by the Farmers Home Administration (FmHA) of the Department of Agriculture (International Center for Social Gerontology, 1979; Tibbitts, 1977; Lawton, 1980; Gray Panthers, 1980). These

| Activity | | | Client income | | Rent subsidy |
Construction	Rehabilitation	Purchase	Limits	Low to moderate	Use of Section 8
yes	yes	no	no	yes	yes
yes	yes	no	no	yes	yes
yes	yes	no	no	yes, with Sec. 8	yes
yes	yes	yes	no	maybe	no
yes	yes	no	yes	yes	yes
yes	yes	no	yes	yes	yes
yes	yes	for existing unit	yes	yes	—

programs are reviewed in this work, but the reader is advised to contact a federal information center for a current report because relevant legislation, appropriations, and regulations change frequently.

Maintenance and Repair Programs

Although about nine-tenths of older Americans reside in independent, unplanned communities, the focus of housing assistance programs has been on new construction of planned projects. The new construction programs have been effective, but many older persons would prefer to remain in their old homes if maintenance and repair assistance were available (Lawton, 1980).

Several programs do provide for help of this type, but "none is available to needy persons in all locations" (Lawton, 1980: 72). Two HUD programs that provide funding for such services are Section 312 and the Community Development Block Grant Program (CDBGP). Section 312 provides low-interest loans for the rehabilitation of substandard housing to bring it up to local building code requirements. Preference for loans is given to low- and moderate-income families, and the program is available only in selected target areas in urban settings (Gray Panthers, 1980; Lawton, 1980). The CDBGP gives funds to local and county governments in designated urban areas and counties. Considerable local discretion is permitted in the use of funds, although housing rehabilitation is one of several priority areas. Other applications of the program include capital improvements, historic preservation, and demolition (Gray Panthers, 1980; Lawton, 1980; International Center for Social Gerontology, 1979). Neither the "312" nor the CDBGP is specifically directed toward older persons.

The Farmers Home Administration also provides loans and grants for housing rehabilitation under Section 504. This program is directed toward older persons whose income is inadequate to pay for repairs needed to remove health and safety hazards. (Funds may be used for other improvements when health and safety hazards are removed at the same time.) Section 504 loans may be made in amounts of up to $7500 and are repayable over 20 years. Outright grants may be made when the Farmers Home Administration determines that the grantee is too poor to repay a loan or that the applicant's income level and the extent of repairs needed suggest that both a loan and a grant are needed. FmHA programs may be used only in communities of 20,000 or less that are outside of standard metropolitan statistical areas or in communities of 10,000 or less that are rural in character but fall within a standard metropolitan statistical area. In addition, applicants must demonstrate that loans are not available from any other source.

Title III (Community Services) of the Older Americans Act may provide for home repairs if they are part of state or area plans. This is subject to local priorities, as described in Chapter 3 of this book. By law, Older Americans Act programs are available to *all* persons age 60 and over, although efforts are made to target services toward the most needy (U.S. DHEW, 1977, 1979). Title XX Social Security Act funds have been used for home repairs, again depending on state and local priorities. Before fiscal year 1982, 45 states provided for some home repairs in their Title XX service plans, but these services were not available in all communities within those states. Title XX eligibility included a means test, which varied from state to state within a range specified in federal regulations (U.S. DHEW, 1978; Gray Panthers, 1980). The block grant program that incorporated previous Title XX activities in fiscal year 1982 permitted continuation of home repair programs.

The Community Services Administration previously provided assistance to low-income families under the Emergency Energy Conservation Program in conjunction with the U.S. Department of Energy. Assistance included grants to household members for assistance with fuel costs and for insulation, storm windows, weatherstripping, and heating system improvements. The goals of the program were to improve the quality of housing in order to reduce energy consumption and to ensure adequate levels of heat for protection of health in cold climates (Gray Panthers, 1980). Some states have elected to continue this type of program with discretionary block grant funds.

Rent Supplement Programs

The U.S. Housing Act of 1937 provides financial aid to state and local housing authorities so they can acquire and manage low-income housing projects. Housing units may be obtained through new construction, through the purchase of existing housing, or through the leasing of existing housing. The act has been amended a number of times since it first recognized the elderly as a population with special housing needs in 1956. At the federal level, the program is administered by HUD. Rents are based on a sliding scale, with a maximum rent of 25 percent of total income up to the local eligibility income limit (Lawton, 1980; International Center for Social Gerontology, 1979; Federal Council on Aging, 1975).

Section 8 of the Housing and Community Development Act of 1974 has been the principal source of rent-supplemented housing for older persons in recent years. It may be used in conjunction with mortgage insurance and direct loan programs under the sponsorship of private enterprises, public agencies, or nonprofit organizations. Section 8 funds make up the difference of between 15 and 25 percent of a household's income (the percentage depends on the relationship of household income to state median income) and the market-value rent of the property (International Center for Social Gerontology, 1979; Gray Panthers, 1980). Legislative changes proposed for fiscal year 1983 included a more restrictive means test for Section 8 eligibility and an increase in the rent-to-income ratio to 30 percent (Leadership Council of Aging Organizations, 1982).

Mortgage Insurance

Insured mortgage loans, provided under Section 231 for all types of housing sponsors, may be combined with Section 8 rent subsidies. Loans may be used only for construction of new facilities or for rehabilitation of facilities already owned by the sponsor. There is no means test for residents of "231" projects with the exception of the one connected with use of Section 8 rent subsidies (International Center for Social Gerontology, 1979).

Direct Loans

The basic HUD direct loan program for housing for the aged is referred to as Section 202. The "202" program was temporarily dropped in 1967 but was revived in 1974 with a small-interest subsidy and can be combined with Section 8 rent supplements. Direct long-term loans are provided to nonprofit sponsors such as churches, unions, and fraternal organizations. Public agencies may not receive funds for housing under this program. Funds are to be used for new construction or rehabilitation but not for the acquisition of existing housing units. Designs under "202" must provide for access to a range of supportive services, although services may not be paid for out of HUD loan funds. Tenants must be either age 62 or above or else handicapped and must have incomes under 80 percent of the local median income adjusted for family size.

The Farmers Home Administration also administers a direct loan program known as Section 515, Rural Rental Housing (RRH). RRH loans may be made to individuals, public or private nonprofit corporations, public bodies, and profit-making companies. Direct loans are made at the going market interest rate, and elderly tenants have no limitations on income or assets except those related to Section 8, which may be used in conjunction with RRH projects. The community size eligibility requirements are the same as those described for the FmHA Section 504 repair and renovation program (International Center for Gerontology, 1970; Gray Panthers, 1980).

Congregate Housing

Congregate housing is distinguished from other types of housing in that such facilities have a central kitchen, a dining room, and provision for delivery of supportive services. Although certain HUD programs have funded congregate facilities since 1970, costs of services were not provided prior to 1978. The Congregate Housing

Services Act of 1978 permitted use of HUD funds for service provision for the first time. The appropriation level for this program has been quite low, and it is viewed as a demonstration rather than a full-scale program. Prior to the 1978 legislation, services in HUD-sponsored facilities were financed through fees, private funds, and programs such as the Older Americans Act and Title XX of the Social Security Act (International Center for Social Gerontology, 1977; Donahue, Thompson, and Curren, 1977; Lawton, 1980).

Shared Housing

Shared housing is one way for the elderly to cope with the high cost of housing, to reduce their loneliness, and to gain a source of assistance and security. The most common form of shared housing is that in which two or more people become house- or apartment-mates. A number of senior citizen organizations participate in "share-a-home" projects that link potential home-mates. Although some older persons value their privacy and exclusive rights to their home too highly to consider shared housing, the concept is receiving increasing acceptance (Murray, 1979; Lawton, 1980).

A less widely accepted and more complex type of residential arrangement is the cooperative residence, or commune. Under this arrangement, a group of unrelated people live together and share in meal preparation, housekeeping, household maintenance, and financial activities. Although cooperative residences are increasing in visibility, relatively few older persons opt for such arrangements at present. Cultural, social, and economic changes may result in greater participation in the future (Gray Panthers, 1980; Hendricks and Hendricks, 1981; Lawton, 1980).

Summary

The type and the location of housing are major influences on the ability of older persons to remain independent and to maintain a satisfactory quality of life. Most older people in the United States are able to maintain their own households. The single, detached, owner-occupied unit is the usual living arrangement. Only a small proportion of older persons resided in mobile homes as of 1976, but both the number and the proportion were increasing at a substantial rate.

In new or rehabilitated housing, environmental design builds in features to help impaired and vulnerable older persons take care of themselves. Carefully planned facilities that address the social and physical needs of residents are essential to the application of the least-restrictive-environment concept. Housing arrangements with built-in support services for a variety of needs are receiving increasing attention because institutionalization may be avoided or deferred.

Government programs directed toward the housing needs of the elderly cover maintenance and repair, rent subsidies, direct mortgage loans to developers, mortgage insurance, and assisted residential living arrangements. Sponsors of government-assisted projects may be private enterprises, nonprofit organizations, or public agencies, depending on the nature of the project and the population to be served.

Because of the factors of economy, security, and loneliness, shared homes have increased in popularity in recent years. Although many older persons place a high value on retaining the privacy of their own homes, others are finding both financial and social-psychological rewards in shared housing.

References

Atchley, R. C. *The Social Forces in Later Life*, 3rd ed. Belmont, CA: Wadsworth Publishing Co., 1980.

Benedict, R. C. "Integrating Housing and Services for Older Adults." In *A Book of Readings for Use in the ICSG Technical Assistance Project on Housing and Services for Older Adults*. Washington, D.C.: International Center for Social Gerontology, 1979.

Bylund, R. A., N. L. LeRoy, and C. O. Crawford. *Older American Households and Their Housing 1975: A Metro–Non-Metro Comparison*. University Park, PA: The Pennsylvania State University Agricultural Experiment Station, 1980.

Donahue, W. T., M. M. Thompson, and D. J. Curren, eds. *Congregate Housing for Older People*, DHEW Pub. No. (OHD) 77-20284. Washington, D.C.: U.S. Government Printing Office, 1977.

Federal Council on the Aging. *The Interrelationships of Benefit Programs for the Elderly. Appendix I, Handbook of Federal Programs Benefiting the Elderly*. Washington, D.C.: U.S. Government Printing Office, 1975.

Gray Panthers. *The Gray Panther Manual*, Vol. II. Philadelphia: Gray Panthers, 1980.

Hendricks, J., and C. D. Hendricks. *Aging in Mass Society*, 2nd ed. Cambridge, MA: Winthrop Publishers, 1981.

International Center for Social Gerontology. *A Book of Readings for Use in the ICSG Technical Assistance Project on Housing and Services for Older Adults*. Washington, D.C.: International Center for Social Gerontology, 1979.

Lawton, M. P. *Environment and Aging*. Monterey, CA: Brooks/Cole Publishing Co., 1980.

Montgomery, J. "The Housing Patterns of Older Families." *Family Coordinator* 21 (1972): 37–46.

Murray, P. *Shared Homes: A Housing Option for Older People.* Washington, D.C.: International Center for Social Gerontology, 1979.

Tibbitts, C. "Aging in America: Present and Future." Address delivered at California State University, Chico, CA, November 11, 1977.

U.S. Department of Health, Education and Welfare, Administration on Aging. *Program Development Handbook for State and Area Agencies on Residential Repair and Renovation for the Elderly*, DHEW Pub. No. (OHDS) 78-20017. Washington, D.C.: U.S. Government Printing Office, 1977.

_____. *Social Programs under Title XX of the Social Security Act.* Washington, D.C.: Office of Human Development Services, 1978.

_____, Administration on Aging. *Older Americans Act of 1965, as Amended: History and Related Acts*, DHEW Pub. No. (OHDS) 79-20170. Washington, D.C.: U.S. Government Printing Office, 1979.

U.S. Senate, Special Committee on Aging. *Congregate Housing for Older Adults: Assisted Residential Living Combining Shelter and Services.* Washington, D.C.: U.S. Government Printing Office, 1975.

_____, Special Committee on Aging. *The Proposed Fiscal Year 1983 Budget: What It Means for Older Americans.* Washington, D.C.: U.S. Government Printing Office, 1982.

White House Conference on Aging. *Housing the Elderly: Background and Issues.* Washington, D.C.: White House Conference on Aging, 1971.

_____. *Toward a National Policy on Aging: Proceedings of the 1971 White House Conference on Aging*, Vol. II. Washington, D.C.: U.S. Government Printing Office, 1973.

_____. *Final Report of the 1981 White House Conference on Aging. Vol. 2, Process Proceedings.* Washington, D.C.: White House Conference on Aging, no date.

Wilson, A. J. E., III. "Effects of Health Problems on the Family Life of Older People." In *Health and the Family*, ed. C. O. Crawford, pp. 203–215. New York: Macmillan Co., 1971.

Chapter

8

Supportive
Services

As the name implies, supportive services are designed to support efforts of older persons to maintain optimal levels of activity, social involvement, and independence. The availability of community-based supports may be critical to quality of life and may make the difference between continued community residence and institutionalization (Harbert and Ginsberg, 1979; Lawton, 1980; Atchley, 1980). In a sense, most of the services discussed in this book may be considered to be supportive. Indeed, the 1981 Older Americans Act amendments substituted the term "supportive services" for "social services" (U.S. Congress, 1982). Access, nutrition, health, home chore, and housing services certainly reinforce efforts of the elderly to maintain levels of activity and independence. This chapter focuses on services that help to fill in the continuum outlined in Chapter 2. Included are (1) nutrition, including congregate meals, home-delivered meals, and nutrition education; (2) home health, personal care, and home help services; (3) counseling and casework services; (4) protective services; (5) legal services; (6) advocacy services to promote the interests of individuals (personal advocacy) and to provide support for policies and issues (issue advocacy); (7) friendly visiting and telephone reassurance services; (8) adult day care; and (9) peer support services, which emphasize mutual support on the part of older persons. (Peer support may also be the means of providing other services such as telephone reassurance.)

Nutrition Services

Lifelong nutritional status affects both one's probability of surviving to old age and one's overall health in old age. The literature on nutrition includes substantial evidence that: (1) food patterns established in early life are retained in later years; (2) lifelong nutritional practices contribute to the development of chronic conditions such as cardiovascular disease, diabetes, and cancer; (3) dietary practices can alter the course and symptoms of certain chronic conditions; (4) a high proportion of the elderly practice poor dietary habits; (5) the level of knowlege about nutrition is low among older persons; and (6) food serves functions other than that of nourishing the body (Wilson, 1981; U.S. DHHS, 1981; Bass et al., 1979; Butler, 1977; Rockstein and Sussman, 1976; Pinellas County Health Department, 1964).

By the time the Older Americans Act was passed in 1965, research findings on nutrition and aging were beginning to accumulate, and various types of home-delivered meals, congregate meals, and nutrition education programs were underway. Sponsors included church groups, voluntary agencies, profit-making caterers, neighborhood service centers, health departments, and dietetic associations (Carter and Webber, 1966). These efforts were limited and inconsistent, but they did call attention to the need for nutritional services. During the late 1960s and early 1970s, the Administration on Aging focused on nutrition projects in its research-and-demonstration component. Demonstration projects conducted throughout the country provided the agency with convincing evidence of the need for a national nutrition program for older persons (U.S. DHEW, 1971, 1972a).

The delegate work book for the 1971 White House Conference on Aging pointed out that food meets social and psychological as well as physiological needs, that adequate and appropriate nutrition can delay the onset of age-related degenerative changes, and that increased attention should be paid to education and research on practical nutrition (White House Conference on Aging, 1971). The Conference recommendations included allocation of federal funds for programs to correct malnourishment, the provision of nutrition education for consumers and service providers, the provision of sufficient funds or supplements to older persons to permit adequate nutrition, and the establishment of the equivalent of a school lunch program for older persons of all income levels (White House Conference on Aging, 1973). In response to the growing support for a national nutrition program, Congress passed legislation in 1972 that became part of the Older Americans Act with the 1973 amendments. From 1973 until 1978, this nutrition legislation was referred to as

Title VII. The 1978 amendments reorganized programs under the Older Americans Act, and the previous Title VII became Title III-C. (People who were involved in the program prior to 1978 still tend to refer to the Older Americans Act nutrition program as the Title VII program.)

Three general types of nutrition service programs for the elderly have evolved. These are congregate meals, home-delivered meals, and nutrition education. Education programs are conducted independently and in conjunction with meal programs.

Older Americans Act Congregate Meal Program

The "Findings and Purpose" statement of Title VII includes the following:

> (a) The Congress finds that the research and development nutrition projects for the elderly . . . have demonstrated the effectiveness of, and the need for, permanent nationwide projects to assist in meeting the nutritional and social needs of millions of persons aged sixty or older. Many elderly persons do not eat adequately because (1) they cannot afford to do so; (2) they lack the skills to select and prepare nourishing and well-balanced meals; (3) they have limited mobility which may impair their capacity to shop and cook for themselves; and (4) they have feelings of rejection and loneliness which obliterate the incentive necessary to prepare and eat a meal alone. These and other physiological, psychological, social, and economic changes that occur with aging result in a pattern of living which causes malnutrition and further physical and mental deterioration (U.S. DHEW, 1974: pp. 43–44).

This statement summarizes concisely the principal concerns and recommendations derived from research and demonstration efforts and from the 1971 White House Conference on Aging. The statement in Title VII went on to recognize that food stamps, commodity foods, and income supplements had helped but could not fully meet identified needs. In view of this, it was legislated that a national congregate meal program be established to serve nutritionally sound meals in a group setting in order to reduce isolation, to encourage social participation, and to provide opportunities for the delivery of supportive social, health, and educational services in conjunction with the meals (U.S. DHEW, 1974). Meeting the objectives of the act required getting older persons, especially those who were socially and psychologically isolated, out of their homes and into sites that facilitated social participation and provided access to other supportive services. Therefore, home-delivered meals were not to be part of the program except for cases in which a regular participant was temporarily unable to attend because of illness. The regulations specified that no more than 10 percent of the meals under Title VII could be home delivered. The program was well received by the general public and by politicians and enjoyed steady growth in appropriations during the 1970s and early 1980s (Kerschner Associates, 1979; U.S. Congress, 1982). By 1977, the number of meals served per year had reached 100 million; by 1979, 150 million; and by 1980, 167 million, including 40 million home-delivered meals (U.S. DHHS, 1981). The restrictions on home-delivered meals were first informally and later formally relaxed; the revised nutrition programs under Title III-C of the 1978 and 1981 Older Americans Act amendments include a separate appropriation earmarked for home-delivered meals.

Home-Delivered Meals

Prior to the 1978 Older Americans Act amendments, it was the policy of the Administration on Aging to fund meals-on-wheels programs only when other resources were not available. At the discretion of state and area agencies, community service funds could be used for such programs when their plans documented that there was a "gap" in community services or that available resources could not meet the need for home-delivered meals. In the majority of communities, voluntary organizations seemed to be satisfying a large part of the need for home-delivered meals, and many groups took pride in their ability to do so without federal assistance. Some critics suggested that these programs often lacked consistency, standards for nutritional adequacy, and adequate food storage and preservation. When the 1978 Older Americans Act amendments added a separate program of home-delivered meals, organizations already operating meals-on-wheels programs were concerned that the federally supported programs would compete with their privately funded operations or that the federal government would impose rigid regulations that would be dysfunctional and disruptive of their activities. Such fears were expessed strongly at public hearings on the new rules and regulations, and the Administration on Aging tried to accommodate the concerns of private programs. Because the need is great and resources are limited, it appears that the Older Americans Act program has strengthened and improved the private programs, although the debate is continuing.

Title III, Part C, Subpart 2 of the Older Americans Act spells out the criteria for home-delivered meals. Specifically, it calls for at least one meal a day to be delivered at least five days a week and for each meal to meet at least one-third of the recommended daily dietary allowance (U.S. Congress, 1982). Provision of home-delivered meals must be based on an assessment of need for such service, and recipients must be homebound because of illness or impairment or otherwise unable to participate in congregate meal programs. The program is administered through the area agency on aging network. Preference for grant awards is given to existing congregate meal providers that have demonstrated their capability for operating the program and to existing public and private nonprofit and voluntary organizations that have demonstrated their capability and that will agree to continue their efforts to obtain support from other sources rather than replace such funds with federal funds (U.S. DHEW, 1980).

Nutrition Education

Nutrition education services are provided for people of all ages through activities of the General Extension Service of the Department of Agriculture, through professional organizations such as the American Dietetic Association, and through voluntary organizations—especially those concerned with nutrition-related diseases, such as diabetes or heart disease. Nutrition courses are also offered through health departments, public schools, colleges and universities, and adult education programs. The Older Americans Act includes a requirement that nutrition education be provided in conjunction with meal programs (U.S. DHEW, 1980). Newspapers, radio, and television are often used to transmit nutrition information to the public. The media can and do provide sound and relevant material; they also serve various special interests through promotional and advertising campaigns, some of which may mislead the consumer and foster poor eating habits. Deutsch contends that "no other area of the national health probably is as obsessed by deception and misinformation as nutrition" (1977: 12). Their general lack of knowledge about nutrition makes many older persons prime targets for advertisers of products that may add to rather than lessen nutritional problems (Wilson, 1981).

Home Health, Personal Care, and Homemaker Services

The distinctions among home health, personal care, and home help are not always clear. According to contemporay use of the terms, home health services include skilled nursing, changing of dressings, rehabilitation therapy, administration of injections, and supervision or dispensing of medication. Personal care services help the elderly to get out of bed and to take care of personal hygiene (bathing, dressing, grooming, and eating). Homemaker (sometimes called home-help) services focus on household management, housekeeping, preparation of meals, and related activities (Tibbitts, 1977; Florida Department of Health and Rehabilitative Services, 1980). In practice, service providers may not maintain strict separation of services by these categories. That is, nurses and home health aides may perform some housekeeping services along with nursing and personal care, and homemakers may provide some personal care services. Nurses and therapists, of course, must be licensed, and home health aides must be supervised by licensed health professionals. Homemakers usually work under the guidance of a social worker or nurse, although this varies with the sponsoring agency. Homemaker services are supposed to be limited to home management and light housekeeping; heavy cleaning, furniture rearrangement, and yard work are categorized as home chore services. The actual duties of home health aides, homemakers, and home chore workers may overlap, depending on agency policies, funding sources, requirements of third-party payers, available resources, and client needs (Winston and Wilson, 1977; Lowy, 1979; Tibbitts, 1977; Beattie, 1976).

Counseling and Casework

Counseling services in a social service context are broadly defined as "interactive processes on a one-to-one or group basis wherein a person is provided direct guidance and assistance in the utilization of needed health and social services and help in coping with personal problems through the establishment of a supportive relationship" (Florida Department of Health and Rehabilitative Services, 1980: 32). Counseling is a term that covers activities ranging from provision of information on services to intensive psychotherapy. Simple information dissemination may be carried out by a lay volunteer with limited training; a highly trained psychiatrist is needed in the case of psychotherapy. Most community-based counseling services are somewhere between these extremes and involve an interactive process between a counselor and older individuals or small groups. Social casework (one of several approaches in counseling) may be used in combination with other approaches such as psychotherapy. The social caseworker attempts to clarify the nature of problems, including marital adjustment, intergenerational conflict, isolation and loneliness, economic management, and adjustment to physical impairments or illness. The caseworker may obtain information for and about the client from agencies, medical practitioners, family members, and other sources in order to assess the situation adequately. In the casework process, emphasis is placed on client self-determination and assistance is given to the client so that he or she can develop coping abilities. The counselor may provide information on resources, alternatives, and likely outcomes or may serve as an advocate for the client, but the decisions on courses of action are made by the client (Lowy, 1979). Some counseling and casework principles are applied in case management and also in protective services.

Protective Services

Broadly defined, protective services include the full range of human services with the consent of the client, plus legally enforced supervision that permits an agency or person to provide services *without* the client's consent (U.S. House of Representatives, 1977). There is no consensus in the literature on the definition of protective services, but a common element in the various definitions is "the potential for legal intervention" (Horowitz and Estes, 1974). A congressional working paper on protective services adopts the following description from a report by Edna Wasser:

> Protective service for the aged has come to represent society's way of caring for those of its aging members who have become limited in caring for themselves and who no longer have or never had others to care for them. The service can also be construed as society's efforts to deal with what it might conceive as deviant behavior. It usually refers to elderly who are living within the community (U.S. Senate, 1977: 3).

Although counseling and casework principles are used by protective service workers, the potential for client self-determination is diminished. Protective service clients may resist help, may be incapable of exercising sound judgment, or may be too sick or feeble to initiate action on their own behalf (Horowitz and Estes, 1974). Eisenberg identifies five characteristics that distinguish protective service clients: the client has some degree of judgmental impairment; the client has a low level of functional capacity for activities of daily living and personal self-maintenance; the client resides in a community setting; the client has no personal social resources (family or friends) to provide assistance; and serious consequences are likely to occur in the absence of intervention (1978). The term "serious consequences" refers to exploitation, loss of property, self-abuse, physical deterioration, or unnecessary institutionalization. Protective service caseworkers must have knowledge of laws relative to competency and guardianship and must have the capacity for intensive casework with clients who may be hostile or confused. The goal is to help the client to achieve the highest level of functioning possible in the least restrictive environment.

Legal Services

Legal services for the elderly primarily deal with questions of wills and inheritance, consumer protection, legal competency, guardianship, and conservatorship (Beattie, 1976; U.S. DHEW, 1979). Legal service projects may involve educating the elderly on legal rights and responsibilities, protecting them against fraud and deceptive business practices (consumer protection), supporting paralegals to assist the elderly and reducing or eliminating legal fees if clients meet low-income eligibility requirements.

The Legal Services Corporation

From the mid-1960s until 1974, a national program of legal services for the poor was operated by the Legal Service Office of the Office of Economic Opportunity. In 1974, Congress established the Legal Services Corporation (LSC) as a separate nonprofit organization to administer the national program. The LSC provides funds and technical assistance for local legal service offices, which hire staff attorneys to provide legal assistance on civil matters to poor persons of all ages. For the year ending September 30, 1981, the corporation served about 187,000 people age 60 and over, who comprise between 12 and 13 percent of all LSC clients (Fritz, 1976; Leadership Council of Aging Organizations, 1982; U.S. Congress, 1982). The fiscal year 1983 federal budget requested no additional funding for the LSC, suggesting that necessary legal services for the poor can be provided through social and community service block grants (U.S. Senate, 1982). Critics say that the proposed change would virtually eliminate federally funded legal services for the poor. The Leadership Council of Aging Organizations described the probable impact of the fiscal year 1983 proposal as follows:

what is now a well-coordinated, cost effective system would be replaced by a hodgepodge of redundant groups. The expertise that LSC has developed in the peculiar and often complex world of poverty law would be lost, to be replaced by too few volunteer attorneys with no experience in disability, nutrition, income mintenance or any other arcane areas of law affecting low-income individuals. The kind of independence neces- sary to represent powerless underrepresented people would give way to political control and constraint under block grants, if funding were to be provided at all. All in all, a system that prevails in 85% of its cases would be replaced by one that is untrained, uncoordinated, underfunded and, with respect to many local and state governments, unwanted (1982: 43).

Older Americans Act Legal Services

The controversial Legal Services Corporation is not the only federal source of legal services support for the elderly. In 1975, the Administration on Aging funded 11 legal services Model Projects under Title III of the Older Americans Act. These complemented the approximately 70 legal service projects then funded through state and area agencies with Older Americans Act social service funds. Activi- ties under these projects included training and utilizing paralegals, providing technical assistance to state units on aging, conducting community education programs, and in some instances, supplement- ing services of LSC projects (Fritz, 1976). The 1978 Older Americans Act amendments recognized the contributions of these projects and designated legal services as a priority area for use of social service funds. The 1981 amendments retained legal services as one of the three supportive services priority areas (the other two are access services and in-home services) (U.S. Congress, 1982).

Advocacy

Advocacy is a concept originally used in connection with legal services. An advocate is defined as one who presents or argues for a client's cause. Advocates take a partisan stand on behalf of an individual or a class of individuals or on policy issues. Individual advocacy, sometimes called case advocacy or personal advocacy, may be carried out as part of social casework, particularly in the special situation of protective services. The personal advocate represents an individual in an attempt to obtain services, to appeal decisions that have denied benefits or services, or to protect the client's rights (Lowy, 1979; Harbert and Ginsberg, 1979). The personal advocate must be knowledgeable about the client's characteristics, resources, problems, and needs. The advocate must also understand agency regulations and laws pertaining to civil rights, benefit programs, and due process (Harbert and Ginsberg, 1979).

Issue advocacy entails taking stands on and promoting public policy relative to an issue affecting large segments of society. Area agencies on aging, state units on aging, and the Administration on Aging are charged with serving as issue advocates for the older population. Voluntary organizations such as the American Association of Retired Persons, the Gray Panthers, the National Caucus on Black Aged, and the National Council on the Aging also engage in issue advocacy. Issue advocates collect and analyze information, develop positions on issues, and provide leadership in order to obtain support for those positions. For example, the Gray Panthers recently published a guide to advocacy that presents extensive documentation for their positions on income maintenance, housing, health care financing, and other areas. The Administration on Aging has established advocacy assistance support centers to provide documentation and technical assistance for state and area agencies in their advocacy efforts; and the American Association of Retired Persons maintains a legislative council that generates policy statements on issues such as health care, consumer protection, and adult education (Gray Panthers, 1980; U.S. DHHS, 1980; NRTA-AARP, 1979).

Lowy suggests three strategies for bringing about change through advocacy: the empirical-rational, the normative-reeducative, and the power-coercive (1979: 411). The empirical-rational approach uses the collection and dissemination of data, expert testimony, conferences with other agencies, education, demonstration projects, and direct contacts with elected officials. This model operates under the assumption that if a proposed change is rationally justified and in the best interests of the community or nation, it will receive support. The normative-reeducative approach uses coalition groups and client groups to raise consciousness and to change attitudes. The power-coercive strategy emphasizes the use of political and moral power to achieve change. Techniques applied include taking stands on issues, circulating petitions, persisting in demands on officials (in Lowy's words, "bombarding officials and legislators and going beyond the usual channels of appeal"), and staging various types of public demonstrations (picketing, marching, street dramas, etc.).

Friendly Visiting and Telephone Reassurance

Beattie describes friendly visiting as one of the oldest volunteer social service programs contributing to increased feelings of security and psychological well-being of the elderly. Historically, the informal network of neighbors and friends provided support through personal visits and, more recently, through telephone visits. These previously informal programs have become part of the formal service delivery system under the sponsorship of voluntary and public agencies and are now provided by both informal and formal systems (Beattie, 1976). Volunteers often perform these functions for agencies, with training, guidelines, and coordination provided by a professional staff member. Friendly visitor volunteers are trained to recognize potential problems and to report these to their supervisors so that appropriate intervention may be initiated. Telephone reassurance programs do not have the advantage of face-to-face contact, but more frequent contacts may be made. The formal telephone reassurance concept is directed toward vulnerable or high-risk older persons who live alone. As well as meeting needs for social contact, telephone reassurance provides a daily check on the physical and mental status of the aged person. Programs usually involve a daily call at a specified time—if the client does not answer, a house call is made. Depending on the local program structure, the person making the visit may be a relative or neighbor, a member of the police, or a visiting nurse. The Administratin on Aging has developed a concise guide for development of telephone reassurance programs; it is available from the U.S. Government Printing Office (Rogers, 1975).

Adult Day Care

Adult day care centers offer a variety of services that overlap the health and social support categories. Day care may include only socializing, meaningful activity, and a meal, or it may include health and rehabilitative services, personal care, and the full range of services usually associated with multipurpose senior centers (Wilson, 1977; U.S. Senate, 1976). By providing these services, day care centers permit impaired older people to maintain their usual place of residence, thereby avoiding unnecessary institutionalization (Beattie, 1976; Wilson, 1977).

Evaluation studies indicate that day care programs are effective in maintaining functionally impaired older persons in community settings instead of in institutions (U.S. Senate, 1976). Day care recipients in ten programs evaluated for the Senate Special Committee on Aging were found to have levels of impairment comparable to those of nursing home residents. The majority of these recipients had multiple chronic conditions, 28 percent had neurological disorders, 23 percent had partial or total paralysis, and about 25 percent required wheelchairs (U.S. Senate, 1976). Funding for day care centers may come from a variety of sources, with multisource funding being the rule. The Older Americans Act has given increasing support to adult day care since the 1978 amendments emphasized the least-restrictive-environment concept.

Peer Support

Groups of older persons may organize on their own or be organized by a goal-directed professional for the purpose of giving mutual support. Networks of friendly visitors or telephone reassurance workers may be made up of peer groups. Peer support is also used in the health and mental health fields. Older persons selected to participate in a formal program may be trained to provide limited counseling services and to know when to call for professional intervention. Peers are often more accessible and more approachable than professionals and thus can be a valuable adjunct to agency staff (Keller and Hughston, 1981; Harbert and Ginsberg, 1979; Shafer, 1981).

Summary

Supportive services contribute to the maintenance of independence and enhance the quality of life for older persons. This chapter contains descriptions of nutrition, home health, personal care, home help, counseling, casework, legal and protective services, personal and issue advocacy, friendly visiting, telephone reassurance, adult day care, and peer support services. In some cases, these programs overlap with those discussed in other chapters. For example, personal care services are related to assisted residential living arrangements discussed under housing.

Inadequate or inappropriate nutrition throughout life contributes to the onset of and the severity of chronic conditions such as diabetes and cardiovascular diseases. In addition, food is often used as a vehicle for involving persons in social activities, for reducing isolation, and for improving the overall quality of life. Nutrition programs are conducted by a variety of private profit-making and nonprofit organizations, agencies, and informal networks. Activities under the Older Americans Act research-and-demonstration program helped to focus attention on the extensive diet-related needs of older persons and on the effectiveness of programs designed to meet these needs.

Findings from research-and-demonstration projects and from deliber-
ations of the 1971 White House Conference on Aging brought the
nutritional and related needs of older persons into prominence and
contributed to the passage of national legislation on nutrition and
aging in 1972.

Three basic types of nutrition-related services are provided
through both private and government sponsorship. These are congregate meals, home-delivered meals, and nutrition education. Congregate meals provide sound meals, nutrition education, and a way of
overcoming isolation and reaching those persons in need of social and
health services. Home-delivered meals incorporate some of the
functions of congregate meals but are intended for those who are
homebound because of illness or impairment or because of geographic isolation. Nutrition education is offered both in conjunction
with and independent of meal programs. Increased knowledge of
nutritional requirements and the effects of inappropriate nutrition
can result in changes in eating habits and in more effective use of
financial resources. Improved eating habits help to prevent certain
diseases, to reduce the severity of certain diseases, and to upgrade
general health and feelings of well-being.

Although home health, homemaker, and personal care services
differ conceptually, they often overlap in practice (except for those
health-related services that require certification or licensing of the
provider). Registered nurses may perform some nonnursing services
that fall under the homemaker or personal care heading, but
homemakers and personal care workers may not legally give skilled
nursing care. Homemakers perform home management and light
housekeeping duties; heavy cleaning, furniture moving, and yard
work are performed by home chore workers. Personal care, which
involves personal hygiene and eating, is generally provided by home
health aides or personal care workers.

Counseling ranges from simple information-giving to intensive
therapy. Casework is a particular type of counseling that emphasizes
self-determination and the concept of "helping people to help
themselves." Service management and protective services use casework techniques. Protective service clients, however, may be unable
to help themselves or to determine what is best for them and may
need legal intervention. Legal services for older persons deal mainly
with questions of wills and inheritance, consumer protection, competency, and education on legal matters. Advocacy services promote the
cause of an individual or group. Issue advocacy may include taking a
stand on and promoting certain policy decisions or legislation.

Friendly visitors and telephone reassurance programs help to
fulfill the elderly's needs for social interaction while serving as a check
on the status of vulnerable older persons. Peer support systems are

often formed to give services of this type as well as lower-level counseling services.

Adult day care centers cover a range of social and health services, including supervision and protection of frail or vulnerable older persons. Although day care centers may be viewed as a setting rather than a service, the center concept generally implies the availability of a package of supportive services designed to permit impaired older persons to maintain community residences.

Most communities provide most of the services reviewed here for at least a part of the older population. Very few places, if any, have the full continuum in all neighborhoods and for all older persons. Supportive services increase the alternatives available to older persons having various degrees of impairment and promote the maintenance of the least restrictive environment.

References

Atchley, R. C. *The Social Forces in Later Life*, 3rd ed. Belmont, CA: Wadsworth Publishing Co., 1980.

Bass, M. A., L. Wakefield, and K. Kolasa. *Community Nutrition and Individual Food Behavior*. Minneapolis, MN: Burgess Publishers, 1979.

Beattie, W. M., Jr. "Aging and the Social Services." In *Handbook of Aging and the Social Sciences*, eds. R. H. Binstock and E. Shanas, pp. 619–642. New York: Van Nostrand Reinhold Co., 1976.

Butler, R. N. *Nutrition and Aging*. Washington, D.C.: U.S. Government Printing Office, 1977.

Carter, H. W., and I. L. Webber. *The Aged and Chronic Disease*. Jacksonville, FL: Florida State Board of Health, 1966.

Deutsch, M. *The New Nuts Among the Berries*. Palo Alto, CA: Bull Publishing Co., 1977.

Eisenberg, D. M. *A Guide for Developing Protective Services for Older Adults*. Harrisburg, PA: Pennsylvania Department of Public Welfare, 1978.

Florida Department of Health and Rehabilitative Services. *State Plan on Aging Under Title III of the Older Americans Act for Florida, Fiscal Years 1981–83*. Tallahassee, FL: State of Florida, 1980.

Fritz, D. "AoA Launches National Legal Services Effort." *Aging* (January, 1976): 1–5.

Gray Panthers. *The Gray Panther Manual*, Vol. II. Philadelphia: Gray Panthers, 1980.

Harbert, A. S., and L. H. Ginsberg. *Human Services for Older Adults: Concepts and Skills*. Belmont, CA: Wadsworth Publishing Co., 1979.

Horowitz, G., and C. Estes. *Protective Services for the Aged*. Washington, D.C.: U.S. Government Printing Office, 1974.

Keller, J. F., and G. A. Hughston. *Counseling the Elderly*. New York: Harper and Row Publishers, 1981.

Kirschner Associates and Opinion Research Corp. *Longitudinal Evaluation of the National Nutrition Program for the Elderly* (executive summary). Washington, D.C.: U.S. Government Printing Office, 1979.

Lawton, M. P. *Environment and Aging*. Monterey, CA: Brooks/Cole Publishing Co., 1980.

Leadership Council of Aging Organizations. "The Administration's 1983 Budget: A Critical View from an Aging Perspective." Unpublished paper, 1982.

Lowy, L. *Social Work with the Aged*. New York: Harper and Row Publishers, 1979.

National Retired Teachers Association/American Association of Retired Persons. *1979 Federal and State Legislative Programs*. Washington, D.C.: NRTA-AARP, 1979.

Philadelphia Geriatric Center. *A Service Management Manual*. Philadelphia, PA: Philadelphia Geriatric Center, 1977.

Pinellas County Health Department and Florida State Board of Health. *Final Report of a Study of Extra-Hospital Nursing Needs in a Retirement Area*. St. Petersburg, FL: Pinellas County Health Department, 1964.

Rao, D. B. "Problems of Nutrition in the Aged." *Journal of the American Geriatrics Society* 21 (1973): 362–367.

Rockstein, M., and M. Sussman, eds. *Nutrition, Longevity, and Aging*. New York: Academic Press, 1976.

Rogers, Virginia. *Guidelines for a Telephone Reassurance Program*, DHEW Pub. (OHD) 75-20200. Washington, D.C.: U.S. Government Printing Office, 1975.

Shafer, E. H. *How to Be Happy though Retired*. Clearwater, FL: Senior Citizens Services, 1981.

Tibbitts, C. "Introduction." In *Ethical Considerations in Long Term Care*, eds. W. E. Winston and A. J. E. Wilson III, pp. 1–16. St. Petersburg, FL: Eckerd College Gerontology Center, 1977.

U.S. Congress, Committee on Education and Labor. *Compilation of the Older Americans Act of 1965 and Related Provisions of Law as Amended through December 29, 1981*. Washington, D.C.: U.S. Government Printing Office, 1982.

U.S. Department of Health and Human Services, Administration on Aging. *Guide to Administration on Aging Programs*, DHHS Pub. No. (OHDS) 80-20176. Washington, D.C.: U.S. Government Printing Office, 1980.

———, Administration on Aging. "Older Americans Month May, 1981, Information Package." Washington, D.C.: AoA, 1981.

U.S. Department of Health, Education and Welfare, Administration on Aging. *Evaluation of Research and Demonstration Nutrition Projects* (advance report for administrative use). Washington, D.C.: AoA, 1971.

———. "Nutrition Programs for the Elderly: Rules and Regulations." *Federal Register*, Vol. 37, No. 162, August 19, 1972a, pp. 16844–16850.

———, Administration on Aging. *A Study of Home Delivered Meals in the United States* (advance report for administrative use). Washington, D.C.: AoA, 1972b.

———, Administration on Aging. *Older Americans Act of 1965 as Amended:*

History and Related Acts, DHEW Pub. No. (OHDS) 79-20170. Washington, D.C.: U.S. Government Printing Office, 1974.

_____, Administration on Aging. "Grants for State and Community Programs on Aging: Rules and Regulations." *Federal Register*, Vol. 45, No. 63, March 31, 1980, pp. 2126–2166.

U.S. House of Representatives, Select Committee on Aging. *Elder Abuse: The Hidden Problem*. Washington, D.C.: U.S. Government Printing Office, 1980.

U.S. Senate, Special Committee on Aging. *Protective Services for the Elderly: A Working Paper*. Washington, D.C.: U.S. Government Printing Office, 1977.

_____, Special Committee on Aging. *Nursing Home Care in the United States: Failure in Public Policy*. Washington, D.C.: U.S. Government Printing Office, 1974.

_____, Special Committee on Aging. *Adult Day Facilities for Treatment, Health Care, and Related Services*. Washington, D.C.: U.S. Government Printing Office, 1976.

_____, Special Committee on Aging. *Developments in Aging: 1978, Part I*. Washington, D.C.: U.S. Government Printing Office, 1979.

_____, Special Committee on Aging. *The Proposed Fiscal Year 1983 Budget: What It Means for Older Americans*. Washington, D.C.: U.S. Government Printing Office, 1982.

White House Conference on Aging. *Delegate Work Book on Nutrition*. Washington, D.C.: White House Conference on Aging, 1971.

_____. *Toward a National Policy on Aging: Proceedings of the 1971 White House Conference on Aging*, Vols. I and II. Washington, D.C.: U.S. Government Printing Office, 1973.

Wilson, A. J. E., III. "Current Needs and Utilization." In *Ethical Considerations in Long Term Care*, eds. W. E. Winston and A. J. E. Wilson III, pp. 31–43. St. Petersburg, FL: Eckerd College Gerontology Center, 1977.

_____. "Sociological Aspects of Nutrition and Aging." In *Handbook of Geriatric Nutrition*, eds. J. H. Hsu and R. Davis. Park Ridge, NJ: Noyes Publishing Co., 1981.

Winston, W. E., and A. J. E. Wilson III, eds. *Ethical Considerations in Long Term Care*. St. Petersburg, FL: Eckerd College Gerontology Center, 1977.

Chapter

9

Training and Education

Training and education services for older persons may be classified in several different ways, some of which are duration, level, setting, and purpose. Duration is the length of contact in terms of hours, months, or years. The level of training may be anywhere on a continuum from basic literacy development (reading and writing) through graduate and professional programs. Training and education may take place at public or technical schools, colleges, senior centers, public meeting facilities under private or public sponsorship (for example, a library, a shopping center or bank community meeting room, a government office), service agencies, housing projects, and nursing homes. Purposes of training and education also cover a wide range, but three broad categories are emphasized: preparation for employment; preparation for provision of care or services to self, family, or peers; and continued personal development.

Participation Rates of Older Persons

Because of the diversity in duration, levels, settings, and purposes, the extent of participation by older people in training and education activities is difficult to determine. Information available from surveys and agency reports suggests that the overall level of participation is low, but that it has been increasing. The formal education system is beginning to offer specialized programs for "nontraditional" students, a term that includes older persons, displaced homemakers, and other population segments that have had lower rates of participation in formal education in the past. Because of demographic trends (changing age structure of the population), reduction of negative stereotypes regarding the ability of the aged to learn, and the positive orientation of the older population toward education and work, it is predicted that older persons will continue the trend toward greater use of educational services (Tibbitts, 1977, 1979; U.S. DHHS, 1981; Ansello and Hayslip, 1979).

Adult education is defined by the U.S. Department of Education as "organized learning to meet the unique needs of persons beyond compulsory school age who have terminated or interrupted their normal schooling. Courses taken by full-time students in high school or college as part of their regular curriculum were not to be reported as adult education" (U.S. DHHS, 1981: 7). The Administration on Aging reports that between 1969 and 1979 there was an increase of nearly 80 percent in the number of people age 55 and over participating in adult education activities as defined above. Part of this increase in numbers is, of course, related to population growth. In terms of rates, the Administration on Aging reports that the proportion of all persons age 55 and over who participated in adult education increased from 2.9 percent in 1969 to 4.4 percent in 1978. The Administration on Aging's analysis of data from the Department of Education and other sources provides some information on the characteristics and goals of older participants in adult education programs. Participation rates were higher for females than for males, for whites than for nonwhites, and for suburban residents than for either central city or rural residents. Participants were more likely to have relatively high incomes and higher levels of educational attainment than nonparticipants. For persons between the ages of 55 and 65, the purpose of education was equally divided between employment and personal/social reasons. For those age 65 and above, a higher proportion (about two-thirds) indicated personal/social reasons. The most popular courses (in rank order) were (1) crafts, (2) business administration and real estate, (3) arts (such as dancing and painting), (4) health care, and (5) home economics. Most of the courses (87 percent) taken by older persons were noncredit. Older persons or their families paid for about 50 percent of costs, public funding paid for about 25 percent, and the remaining 25 percent came from a variety of private sources (U.S. DHHS, 1981).

An analysis by Hess and Markson (1980) of data from the *Monthly Labor Review* showed substantial rates of participation in formal school programs by persons beyond the customary school age in 1976. However, these data are for all persons age 35 and over and are not divided by age category to show rates for the 55-plus or the 65-plus age groups. About 1,600,000 persons age 35 and above were reported to be attending some type of school. Of these, almost three-fourths were attending college, the majority on a full-time basis. An additional 22 percent attended trade or vocational schools, and about 4 percent attended elementary or high schools. These figures include only enrollment in traditional school settings. Hendricks (1982) reports that over three million persons age 40 and over were enrolled in some form of organized education in 1977.

A 1975 California study revealed that very few older persons were enrolled in the formal university system. Higher rates of involvement were reported in extension, continuing education, and external degree programs, but these were still low compared to those of other age groups. Barriers to increased participation by older Californians included shortage of off-campus learning opportunities, lack of appropriate counseling, lack of transportation, indifference of faculty and staff to the needs of older adults, and relatively high fees (California Office on Aging, 1975).

A study by the Adult Education Association, as reported by Atchley (1980), provided additional support for some of the information described above. This study of 3500 programs serving older persons concluded that most courses were taught in classroom settings, support services were inadequate, and older persons preferred programs adapted to their lifestyles and special needs. Although most courses were taught in classrooms, they were not necessarily in schools or under school sponsorship. About two-thirds of the courses were offered through senior centers, libraries, extension services, and recreation departments rather than through public school systems and colleges; most of the programs were of recent origin.

Recent developments suggest that specialized programs for older persons will continue to increase. Many postsecondary institutions, concerned about declining enrollment as the "baby boom" cohort moves into middle age, are beginning to look to the older population as a source of students (Hess and Markson, 1980; Atchley, 1980; U.S. Senate, 1979). Free or reduced tuition, special short courses, and summer workshops are some of the approaches being used to attract older persons to college campuses. The majority of university systems now provide for either reduced fees or free enrollment for older persons. Community colleges in most states have begun concerted efforts to develop programs tailored to the needs of older persons.

Special Programs for Older Persons

Federal Agency Programs

The Senate Special Committee on Aging reports that approximately 50 federal programs are authorized to provide educational opportunities for older persons. The Department of Education (formerly the Office of Education), the Administration on Aging, the Department of Labor, and the National Center for Voluntary Action (ACTION) are the major agencies involved. Under Title I of the Higher Education Act, the Department of Education provided programs that ranged from preparation for employment to arts and crafts. Older persons often helped to teach these programs. The federal budget proposal for fiscal year 1983 eliminated the Department of Education and Title I funding, but initiated a new "foundation for educational assistance." This foundation is to administer a program of block grants and consolidated aid for state and local educational activities (U.S. Senate, 1982).

The Department of Education and the Administration on Aging have provided funding for pre- and post-retirement training, and for training older persons to provide services for their peers. ACTION trains older persons for participation in volunteer activities, and the Department of Labor provides training in connection with certain employment programs (U.S. Senate, 1979).

The Elderhostel Program

One of the innovative programs sponsored by institutions of higher learning is the "elderhostel" program, which was initiated by the New England Center for Continuing Education in 1975. This program involves a network of participating colleges and universities that offer low-cost residential short courses for the elderly during the summer months. Participants may visit a different elderhostel campus each summer or may visit several during the same summer, taking one-week courses covering a wide range of topics. In 1980, over 300 colleges and universities throughout the nation joined in the program (Atchley, 1980; Elderhostel, 1980; Tenenbaum, 1979). The elderhostel program was initiated with federal assistance, but currently is supported through local funds, fees, and contributions (U.S. Senate, 1982).

Lifetime Learning

The United States Office of Education defines lifetime learning as "the process by which individuals continue to develop their knowledge, skills, and attitudes over their lifetimes" (U.S. Senate, 1979). The process includes training, employment, and volunteer work as learning experiences; it is not limited to traditional concepts of education. Several voluntary organizations have become involved in lifetime learning projects. The most widely known and the first to apply the name is the nationwide Institute of Lifetime Learning, sponsored by the National Retired Teachers Association/American Association of Retired Persons (NRTA-AARP).

The NRTA-AARP Institute staff works with educational institutions, state and local governments, and older persons to stimulate interest in the development of educational opportunities for older persons. It also collaborates and provides technical assistance to local NRTA and AARP chapters so they can develop a variety of noncredit courses. In many places, community colleges or universities cosponsor adult and continuing education programs with NRTA-AARP (NRTA-AARP, 1980; U.S. Senate, 1979).

Policy Considerations

NRTA-AARP points out that continuing education is "important to the elderly's quality of life and mental and physical well-being" (1979: 37). Educational programs also help to equip older persons to cope with social and technological change, personal and health problems, and needs for self-fulfillment. In Senate committee testimony in 1978, the National Association of Senior Citizens (NASC) underscored the poor response of adult basic education programs to the needs of older persons:

> Public and privately funded ventures into what is called citizen education (an effort to provide citizens with the information and skills needed to use our democratic political process to better their lives) tend to overlook the aged and concentrate upon the young and middle aged. But the aged—not our members at least—do not retire from citizenship (U.S. Senate, 1979: 24).

The National Committee on Careers for Older Americans suggests that our educational system could be of great assistance to the older population, but that little response has been observed. The 1981 White House Conference on Aging Committee on Education and Training took a strong position, referring to education as "an inherent right of all age groups" (White House Conference on Aging, 1981: 92). Institutions that *have* responded recognize that older persons have legitimate needs for and claims to the services provided. Organizations such as the American Association of Community and Junior Colleges have taken into account the demographic, economic, and social circumstances that affect older persons and the educational system, and they have attempted to adapt their resources to meet the challenge.

The National Committee on Careers for Older Americans made the following policy recommendations:

> (1) Adopt specific objectives for helping older people to prepare for further involvement in economic, social, and cultural activities; (2) assign a high priority for use of institutional time, energy, and resources for the achievement of the agreed-upon objectives; (3) develop a recruiting and counseling program for older people designed to be just as intense and as personalized as the recruiting and counseling program for younger people (1979: 55).

The California study cited earlier also included a set of policy recommendations. These are (paraphrased): (1) increase accessibility of programs by modifying schedules, altering admission policies, adjusting fees, and providing transportation; (2) provide specialized counseling for older adults; (3) use different recruiting and teaching techniques that may be more appropriate for older persons; (4) direct educational programs toward the special needs of older persons; (5) seek involvement of older persons in planning and in teaching; (6) research the specific employment-related needs of older persons (California Office on Aging, 1975).

Thus, the American education system is responding, however slowly, to the needs of the elderly. Responses accelerated in the 1970s, but slowed with federal budget cuts in the early 1980s. The outlook for the future was summed up very well by Clark Tibbitts: "It is likely that institutions, which are finding themselves with surplus resources as the number of young students levels off, will seek to maintain enrollments from among increasingly well-educated, intellectually curious cohorts of middle-aged and older people" (1977: 9).

Summary

Education programs for older persons may be directed toward preparation for employment, development of knowledge and skills for care of self or others, or continued self-development and enhancement of well-being. Although the traditional setting for education is the school classroom, programs for the elderly may take place in a variety of settings, including senior centers, housing projects, agencies, and nursing homes. Some older persons need or want only limited educational experiences; others are interested in long-term intensive study. The educational system has not been responsive to the older population. In recent years, participation rates have increased substantially, but they are still low relative to those of younger persons. Shortage of off-campus learning opportunities, lack of appropriate counseling, disinterested staff, and high costs have been cited as barriers to increased participation by older persons.

A number of specialized programs have been developed through the efforts of federal agencies and voluntary organizations such as NRTA-AARP. Some colleges and universities have begun to respond because of the decrease in the size of the traditional college-age population and the increase in demands for higher education by older adults. Reduced or free tuition for the elderly has been provided on a "space available" basis. The Elderhostel summer program expanded from about 5 participating colleges and universities in 1975 to over 300 in 1980. The lifetime learning concept is gaining increased attention, and the NRTA-AARP Institute of Lifetime Learning continues to expand. The American Association of Community and Junior Colleges has assumed leadership in adapting community programs to the needs of older persons.

References

Ansello, E. F., and B. Hayslip, Jr. "Older Adult Education: Stepchild and Cinderella." In *Gerontology in Higher Education*, eds. H. L. Sterns, E. F. Ansello, B. M. Sprouse, and R. Layfield-Faux, pp. 262–273. Belmont, CA: Wadsworth Publishing Co., 1979.

Atchley, R. *The Social Forces in Later Life.* Belmont, CA: Wadsworth Publishing Co., 1980.

California Office on Aging. *California Higher Education Study for the Aging.* Sacramento, CA: California Office on Aging, 1975.

Elderhostel. *Annual Report, 1979.* Boston: Elderhostel, Inc., 1980.

Estes, C. *The Aging Enterprise.* San Francisco: Jossey-Bass Publishers, 1979.

Hendricks, J. Personal communication, 1982.

Hess, B. B., and E. W. Markson. *Aging and Old Age.* New York: Macmillan and Co., 1980.

National Committee on Careers for Older Americans. *Older Americans: An Untapped Resource.* Washington, D.C.: Academy for Educational Development, 1979.

National Retired Teachers Association/American Association of Retired Persons. *The 1979 Legislative Policy and 1979–80 Joint Legislative Committee Policy Guidelines of the National Retired Teachers Association and the American Association of Retired Persons.* Washington, D.C.: NRTA-AARP, 1979.

_____. *National Community Service Programs.* Washington, D.C.: NRTA-AARP, 1980.

Tenenbaum, F. *Over 55 Is Not Illegal.* Boston: Houghton Mifflin Co., 1979.

Tibbitts, C. "Aging in America: Present and Future." Address delivered at California State University, Chico, CA, November 11, 1977.

_____. "Can We Invalidate Negative Stereotypes of Aging?" *The Gerontologist* 19 (1979): 10–20.

U.S. Department of Health and Human Services, Administration on Aging. *Statistical Notes from the National Clearinghouse on Aging*, No. 6. Washington, D.C.: U.S. Government Printing Office, 1981.

U.S. Department of Health, Education and Welfare, Administration on Aging. *Information Memorandum: Office of Education Act.* Washington, D.C.: U.S. Government Printing Office, August 3, 1979.

U.S. Senate, Special Committee on Aging. *Developments in Aging: 1978, Part I.* Washington, D.C.: U.S. Government Printing Office, 1979.

_____, Special Committee on Aging. *The Proposed Fiscal Year 1983 Budget: What It Means for Older Americans.* Washington, D.C.: U.S. Government Printing Office, 1982.

White House Conference on Aging. *Final Report of the 1981 White House Conference on Aging, Vol. 2, Process Proceedings.* Washington, D.C.: White House Conference on Aging, no date.

Chapter

10

Maintaining the
Dignity of Patients

The following article was prepared by Dr. Wilma Donahue for a conference on Ethical Considerations in Long Term Care carried out by Eckerd College under contract with the Veterans Administration. Although the focus is upon the "patient" in a long-term care setting, much of what Dr. Donahue says is applicable to older persons in any service delivery setting. Her sensitivity to the patient's feelings and value as a person is clearly reflected in this paper, and a review by this author would be very unlikely to capture the Donahue qualities. Thus, she graciously agreed to this reprint.

The October 23rd issue of the *Washington Post* newspaper announced the destruction of a Washington movie theater. The reported said: The Apex Theater is being torn down to be replaced by offices and shops. Its last show has ended and it awaits demolition in a curiously ornate theater. But the fancier Washington movie houses in the middle of town have already been torn down or allowed to deteriorate, and now the Apex, expiring in dignity, seems all the greater loss.

Having been sensitized to the term *dignity* by my assignment today, I wondered why the reporter chose to describe the old Apex as expiring in dignity and so I read on. I learned that in the reporter's mind, the old Apex was distinguished because it had served a worthy purpose and was a commendable part of the history of the flamboyant past of the movies.

Reprinted with permission from *Ethical Considerations in Long Term Care*, eds. W. E. Winston and A. J. E. Wilson III (St. Petersburg, FL: Eckerd College Gerontology Center, under contract with the Veterans Administration, 1977), pp. 157–170.

Dignity

To me, this story seemed to have important parallels to the issue of dignity and old patients. Like the old Apex, these old people may not have achieved high rank, but nonetheless they have made their contribution to the developing society of their communities and the nation. They, too, are distinguished because their lives have been a part of the larger pattern of the history of mankind, and thus, they have attained a quality of dignity which is to be respected as they suffer the indignities of long-term illness and age.

What Is Dignity?

Still, we must ask, what is this thing we call dignity, a quality so often mentioned and so seldom defined? The word derives from the Latin *dignitas*, meaning worth or merit. It includes recognition of one's worth by others and also respect for one's own worthwhileness. It is an attribute often described as innate, as in the common phrase of "man's innate dignity." It is often linked with the term respect, which as a noun means to refrain from the interference with another, that is to respect the rights of another. The concept of dignity is better understood in terms of long-term care situations if we consider its antonym, *indignity*. *Indignity* is defined as something that humiliates, insults, or injures the dignity or self-respect of another. It is an affront to another person, an action which manifests contempt for him.

Dignity Imperiled in Long-Term Care Settings

Why, we ask, is it necessary to identify and deal with issues of patient dignity in a symposium on the ethics of long-term care? The literature contains a number of eloquent statements describing professional and humane ways to treat patients and to preserve their self-respect and dignity. Unfortunately the literature also offers horrifying descriptions of patient abuse and neglect.

The U.S. Senate Special Committee on Aging (1974) has analyzed the complaints against nursing homes which were reported at different times in 14 of the country's leading general newspapers. The complaints fell into 29 categories. Of these categories, the four that were mentioned in 14 of the 15 newspaper stories were untrained and inadequate personnel, absence of doctors, lax enforcement of regulations, and lack of respect for human dignity. The examples given to illustrate the assaults on the dignity of patients were failing to bathe them, thus engendering feelings of guilt and self-disrespect because other patients and visitors were offended by the body odor; scolding and ridiculing patients who make errors; calling maintenance men to help women in and out of baths without regard to the women's embarrassment, sense of modesty, or right of privacy. The list of indignities to the person of the individual is long and all are destructive of self-esteem and contribute to the despair of so many old people.

Dignity—A Patient Right

These distressing circumstances, although far from being found in all long-term care facilities, were found in so many that in 1974 the Department of Health, Education and Welfare deemed it necessary to issue regulations requiring the management of each skilled nursing care facility to establish a list of patients' rights covering at least 14 prescribed rights, policies, and procedures. The ninth of these rights states that the patient is to be "treated with consideration, respect, and full recognition of his dignity and individuality, including privacy in treatment and in care for his personal needs." The patients' bill of rights is equally applicable to any type of facility offering long-term care to the elderly, even if it be within the confines of their own homes.

Age and Worth

But drawing up, printing, and distributing a statement of patients' rights does not guarantee that the quality of care will be materially changed. One prime problem may be seated in the rejection of oldness, an attribute of both animate and inanimate objects which labels them as worthless. From infancy onward, we are constantly learning that age depreciates the value of all things, of all except those which may become valuable because they are a great rarity—a circumstance which does not apply to the American population of 22 million persons aged 65 and over. In the American value system, old men and old women have long since depreciated in worth; in consequence, when they become dependent on others to care for them and to determine in large part the quality of their lives, they are doomed to suffer many indignities from those who consider them to be without value.

Addressing this point, social worker Minna Field (1968), in her book *Aging with Honor and Dignity*, stresses the need to abandon the stereotype of doddering, helpless, and useless old people and to substitute a new concept of aging with competency. She believes that once this new concept is accepted, the younger generation can be taught to appreciate the contributions of their elders. "What we need," she says, "is to concentrate all our efforts to help enhance the dignity of the individual so that he may achieve maximal satisfaction in his later life." Other writers, likewise, pin their hopes on educating the young to bring about changes in attitudes toward and treatment of elderly people. Neugarten (1975) believes that, if the young-old will create an attractive image of aging, they will allay the fears of young people about growing old. On this premise, one might assume that in the future the old may expect more appreciation and less rejection from the society and from those persons whose destiny may include caring for old people as patients. Although such a conclusion may be true, we can scarcely justify failing to improve the quality of life and care of all those millions who will become old and die while the new concepts get in place, while the young are being educated and then grow into attractive young-old people. One ethic (principle) to which we must be committed is that we cannot wait a generation for attitudes toward aging to change—millions of today's old people must be attended now.

Are elderly patients as concerned about their worth and dignity as are the professionals, reformers, and government? Goldfarb answers this question in the affirmative. He finds from his extensive studies that the elderly frequently value being well-regarded as more important than being well cared for. Equally cogent is the observation of a leading geriatric nurse who states that "human regard and good care are inextricably linked and not an either-or proposition" (Kelly, 1975).

Patient Uniqueness and Personalization of Care

The physical and mental frailty of those ill elderly persons who can no longer cope without assistance from others does not extinguish their need for understanding, recognition, and appreciation. Psychiatrist Dr. Jack Weinberg (1976) says, "Each patient has his own and unique life, his own memories, hopes, expectations, habits, and biases. Each has had a responsibility in the management of his own life.... Each has found support, reinforcement, guidance, and correction from loving and perceptive others; and each has suffered from hands of others." To the patient these are the precious ingredients of his uniqueness. But who, we ask, cares in the impersonal environment of an institutional setting? Even if the patient is cared for at home by his family, appreciation for the qualities that have made up his personality may have long ago been forgotten so that now he is perceived only as a family burden.

To personalize care for each person is not simple. It demands understanding and appreciation not only of the patient's unique life experiences and current needs, but also of the demands of the formalized care system. "Long-term institutionalization, whether in a hospital, nursing home for the chronically ill, or a home for the aged, is a stressful and depersonalizing experience. The patient not only has to give up most of the management of his own affairs but also must suffer invasions of his privacy and indignities to his person that are the built-in stresses of professional care" (Kelly, 1975).

Preserving the Patients' Dignity and Worth

What then can be done to provide meaning and dignity to the life of the elderly person while undergoing long-term treatment and care or while waiting and hoping for an early death with as little pain and as much dignity as possible?

Improving Institutional Goals

Obviously, only lecturing staff on the rights of old people is futile. Neither nurses nor any other personnel will significantly improve their attitudes towards patients only by taking courses in ethics, psychology, or the humanities. In fact, some studies show that attitudes toward old people of students taking a first course dealing with the process of aging worsened as a result of their new knowledge.

Any improvement in the quality of care given in an institution requires questioning and reappraising the structure, organization, and hierarchy. Are the personnel correctly paid? Are they listened to by physicians and managers? Are they being encouraged to use their intelligence, imagination, and initiative in their work? Are they themselves respected persons in the care setting? Are they more committed to the needs of the patient as a person than to the efficiency of the nursing routine?

These are goals that can only be achieved by action. To illustrate the point, I want to recall one of many similar experiences the University of Michigan Institute of Gerontology staff had as it developed the technique of milieu therapy for use in long-term care hospitals and nursing homes. The Jackson County hospital was housed in an old 19th century building. It was crowded with indigent chronically ill patients, most of whom would spend the rest of their lives there. The staff was adequate in number with a registered nurse as head. Treatment was strictly custodial, including food, sleeping quarters in dormitories. The staff offered personal service but little more. Permission was given the University workers to convert the hospital into a therapeutic community, a situation in which the environment became a treatment agent substituting rehabilitation for custodial care. The hospital staff was not asked to change its routine or the service it provided patients. After the new program got underway, it soon became obvious to the regular hospital staff that it was far more rewarding to assist patients to restore their capabilities through participation in meaningful activities than to give the traditional dependency-creating care they had been providing. The result was that the staff taught the patients to care for themselves, thus saving staff time enough to take part in the rehablitation activities. The local community took such note and pride in the new program and its effect on reactivating patients that for the first time after trying for years, a bond issue to construct a new county hospital was passed. A beautiful hospital was built with space provided for recreation, socialization, and rehabilitation. A staff professionally prepared to carry on a full program of rehabilitative milieu therapy was employed. And to update this project, 15 years later it stands as an ongoing model for all county hospitals in Michigan. The enthusiasm of the staff is unabated. And basically, it is no more than a program through which the individuality and potential of patients is recognized and supported by encouraging independence and maximum responsibility within their capabilities for their own care.

Good Nursing Principles Related to Human Regard

Cynthia Kelly (1975), a geriatric nurse, has stated formally some principles on good nurse practice which are designed to engender human regard for elderly patients. Her first principle calls for recognizing that every elderly person has a history of accomplishments, strengths, and adaptability that have enabled him to become elderly. To infantilize such a person by taking away his rights and failing to recognize his worth is the first step toward making the patient a non-person. Instead, the application of this first principle of human regard should be the instant involvement of the aged persons with their new environment, the people in it, and the part they can play. Miss Kelly goes on to say that:

> If nurses reverse the traditional approach—assessing the patient to discover what he lacks that they must provide—and make it their first

priority to assess what this person brings with him, what he has to offer, what life experience he has had that can aid them and other residents, life in the new home may be worth living.

The second principle states that the individual is to be regarded as a unique individual, encouraging the preservation of his identity, his sense of control, and his inalienable right to be the chief member of the health team with voice, vote, and veto power. Preserving individuality is composed among others of such measures as helping the patient dress attractively in his own clothes, urging him to choose when a choice exists, allowing the patient to arrange his living space according to his preferences and to include cherished items, arranging for flexible visiting hours, setting times for care routines convenient to the patient rather than to the staff. Rigid insistence on non-essential routines achieves only negative results—patient irritation, staff frustrations, and pitched battles in petty areas.

A third principle requires that every patient should be known as completely as possible. I would interpret this as essential in establishing more than a casual relationship. It is tantamount to becoming a potential confidante if the patient has no other persons to whom to confide. It calls for little more to begin with than learning the patient's present and past dislikes, his general affective state and view of his world, how he earned his living, and whether he found joy in it, who of his family are still living and who have been the most important people in his life. This information provides the basis not only for learning to genuinely like and appreciate the patient but, also, for better understanding of his behavior.

Listen and Understand

Understanding the behavior of old people requires that one understand how the person perceives his reality and what the consequences of this perceived reality are. Dr. Weinberg (1976) points out that no matter what one's experiences may have been, each of us has a need to elaborate upon them—that is, to create the dimensions of our own reality. Dr. Weinberg says that "these elaborations tend to distort the truth, but add to the reality which the individual wishes to convey. . . . What emerges is a romanticized version of events; a dramatization of the facts; the good becomes magnificent, the sad tragic." It is these poetic interpretations of one's experiences that need understanding and interpretation by listeners. Dr. Theodore Copper (1970), Assistant Secretary for Health, Department of Health, Education and Welfare, reports that in talking with patients in different care settings, he finds the thing they complain about most is that no one seems to have time to listen to them. He supports formalized statements of patient's rights, but firmly believes that these agreements cannot substitute for human attention and for understanding of patients by all personnel.

In addition to the elaboration of life experience, there are, according to Dr. Robert Butler (1973), inner reactions to old age, which seem to be a part of the developmental work of late life. "One of these is the life review which takes place through reminiscence accompanied by feelings of nostalgia, regret, pleasure." At an earlier time, Doctors Maurice Linden and Douglas Courtney (1960) elaborated upon this need of old people to reminisce. They saw what they called "retrospective examination" as the task of the last phase of later maturity—a phase which, they believe, is ushered in by an individual's need to correlate the present with the past in order to determine the true nature of one's life accomplishments, errors, and rediscoveries. They point out that the person's cultural vision at this level is at its broadest possible development, embracing one nearly complete life cycle and its relatedness with a multitude of other life cycles throughout the span of existence.

The individual needs to compare and contrast his values with the cultural values to which he has been longitudinally exposed and to go through a process of conscious reasoning to determine meaning and purpose. This evaluation and assessment of the meaning and worth of his life leads the old person to seek confirmation from those around him. Is it not possible that the often repeated reminiscences of past episodes and experiences, so tiresome to the uninterested who must listen, is but the old person's way of affirming his own belief in his worthwhileness, his right to respect, his innate dignity? If this be true, should not our transactional communications reassure and reward with approval those things which he perceives now as the realities of his life? In this way, we can help bring closure to his task of reminiscence and free the old person's mind from concern, thus allowing him to direct his psychic energies to constructive activites of the present—getting well, or adjusting to continuing pain and suffering, or putting his affairs in order, and taking part in the life of his care facility. This implies another principle in the care of elderly patients, that is the creation of an environment that bustles with the activity of its residents.

Environmental Factors and Individuality

A therapeutic ambience of a long-term care facility, as has been pointed out, is not the hospital hubbub—the traffic of staff rounds, examining, treating, and hurrying away—rather it is the normal liveliness of a patient population demonstrating the intense inter-relatedness with others which is so necessary to human health (Kelly, 1975). The description of Hubert Humphrey, recently a cancer patient in a New York hospital, must surely be a prime example of human relatedness. He was reported to be visiting each person on his floor every day, taking the Secretary of State, Mr. Kissinger, to meet each of the patients, distributing the over-abundance of the flowers he received to everyone, sharing his views on the election, and perhaps politicking a bit. Thus, he was contributing not only to his own recuperation but to that of all those other patients suffering the same disease.

An active, busy milieu fulfills other purposes by providing opportunity for participation in new experiences. Each transaction presents a challenge and when it is coped with successfully, the ego is strengthened and the individual's capabilities are enhanced (Cumming and Cumming, 1967).

Perhaps the most important of the socio-environmental factors in long-term care settings related to human dignity is that of privacy—a quality of life cherished by young and old, but all the more so the older the person becomes (Lawton and Bader, 1970). Visual and auditory privacy and autonomy over one's own territory is the prize. In addition to assuring the comfort of being one's own person, the private room symbolizes the continuing worth of the tenant and his right to determine with whom he will share the intimacies of his life (Pastalan, 1970). Studies made of preferences for private or shared rooms in England, Wales, Switzerland, as well as the United States (Townsend, 1962; Lipman, 1968; Noam, 1968; Lawton and Bader, 1970) show that, in these cultures at least, the desire for privacy is essentially universal.

Yet in most long-term care facilities, rooms generally must be shared by two, three, four, or even dozens of persons. At the very time in his life that the elderly individual is least able to fend for himself, he is stripped of privacy and forced to exist in the constant presence of others (Lawton, 1974). Little wonder that many persons defend themselves by withdrawing: the only available escape from the indignities of an intolerable situation they are powerless to change.

The practice of shared rooms is defended on several grounds. Some patients adapt and do not protest so it is assumed that they do not really miss their privacy. Physicians and other professionals argue that the shared room is preferable because it promotes more social interaction. Dr. Butler (1974) does not argue against shared rooms but recommends that roommates each have access to privacy for four hours a day, a circumstance difficult to fulfill in rooms shared by a number of persons, one or more of whom may be bedridden.

Economics, rather than the right of the individual to the dignity of privacy and autonomy, is the dictator of the principle of shared space. The for-profit facilities crowd in patients in order to realize a higher margin of income per room; insurance companies and Medicare and Medicaid will not pay the full cost of a private room; and skyrocketing building costs further complicate the possibility of providing individual quarters at costs that can be afforded. Yet one must ask, can we be sure that most elderly patients might not be happier and healthier living in privacy in a miniscule cubicle—rather than in 40 square feet in a shared room?

Changing Attitudes toward an Ethic of Patient Dignity

Perhaps I have overstressed the seeming lack of social and professional sensititivity and the national concern for the humanistic treatment of the ill elderly. Actually there are many statements reflecting noble intentions and philosophies. Shills (1959), for one, in a chapter on the autonomy of the individual says that "our society professes a fundamental belief in the uniqueness of the individual, in his basic dignity, and as a human being, and on the need to maintain social processes that safeguard his social individuality." Professionals discussing proper patient care urge replacing tender loving care with encouraging patients to undertake self-care. To over-serve the patient, they say, deadens his dignity, initiative, and self worth. Cicero said it in another way—"Old age is respectable just as long as it asserts itself, maintains its proper rights and is not enslaved to anyone."

Organizations and government are proclaiming new intentions to improve the quality of care in long-term settings. In a 1975 study on the improvement of facilities (U.S. Department of Health, Education and Welfare, 1975), the Public Health Service noted that "one of the crucial issues of care in skilled nursing homes is the maximum preservation of each person's life style within the care setting." The report goes on to say that "to implement this concept it is necessary that each individual's life style and psychosocial needs be known by all care personnel . . . so that patient care can be encouraged and supported in the direction of personal and social autonomy."

A 1970 national symposium on patients' rights in health care (Fay, 1970) brought forth such statements as "it astounds me that it is necessary to codify such things as respect for the individual, the right to courtesy, and the right to privacy."

At a 1974 conference on "Long-Term Care Data" (Murnaghan, 1976), it was decided that, in addition to information on diagnoses, there should be added some factor related to personal dignity and quality of life, a surprising statement from statisticians. In the Public Health Service "Forward Plan for Health—FY 1978–1982" (1976), one of the six major themes enumerated is that of quality health care. "Attention to the health-related social, emotional, and environmental needs," the report says, "is crucial to patient satisfaction and to the success of long-term care."

These are all noble sentiments reflecting awareness and good intentions. But it is questionable whether prescription and proclamation alone can dissipate the deep seated personal rejection of aging and agedness and substitute an ethic of dignity which will so permeate the American value system that conscience will automatically inhibit indignities and mistreatment of elderly patients. It will surely take heroic measures of the magnitude of our just completed political campaign, backed by enough funds to reach every citizen, to bring about, in the foreseeable future, a re-examination of the worth to be accorded the old. Should this come about, the old people will win out and an ethic of dignity for both the well and the ill will be firmly established. Such an ethic may well be couched in the words Marcus Aurelius enunciated centuries ago:

Remember this—that there is a proper dignity and proportion to be observed in the performance of every act of life.

References

Butler, R. N., and Lewis, M. I. *Aging and Mental Health: Positive Psychological Approaches*. St. Louis: C. B. Mosby Co., 1973, 202–228.
Cooper, T. "Implementation of Patients' Rights." In *Proceedings: National Symposium on Patients' Rights in Health Care*. Washington, D.C.: U.S. Department of Health, Education and Welfare, Public Health Service, Publication No. (HSA) 76-7002, 1970, 36–39.
Cumming, J., and Cumming, Elaine. *Ego and Milieu: Theory and Practice of Environmental Therapy*. New York: Atherton Press, 1967, 46–57.
Fay, Linda. "Patient-Consumer Advocacy." *Proceedings: National Symposium on Patient's Rights in Health Care*. Washington, D.C.: U.S. Department of Health, Education and Welfare, Public Health Service, Publication No. (HSA) 76-7002, 1970, 25–30.
Field, Minna, and Bluestone, E. M. *Aging with Honor and Dignity*. Springfield, Illinois: Charles C Thomas, 1968.
Kelly, Cynthia N. "Nursing Care." In Cowdy, E. V., and Steinberg, R. U. (eds.), *The Care of the Geriatric Patient*. St. Louis: C. V. Mosby Co, 1975, 368–370.

Lawton, M. P., and Bader, Jeanne. "Wish for Privacy by Young and Old." *Journal of Gerontology*, 1970, 25, Part I, 48–54.

Lawton, M. P. "Coping Behavior and the Environment." In Schwartz, A. N., and Mensch, I. N. (eds.), *Professional Obligations and Approaches to the Aged*. Springfield, Illinois: Charles C Thomas, 1974.

Linden, M., and Courtney, D. "The Human Cycle." In Tibbitts, C., and Donahue, Wilma (eds.), *Aging in Today's Society*. Englewood, N.J.: Prentice-Hall, Inc., 1960, 148–152.

Lipman, A. "A Socio-architectural View of Life in Three Old People's Homes,"*Gerontology Clinica*, 1968, 19, 88–101.

Murnaghan, Jane H. (ed.). *Long Term Care Data*. New York: J. B. Lippincott Co., 1976, 5.

Neugarten, Bernice L. "The Future of the Young-Old." *Gerontologist*, 1975, 15 (No. 1), Part II, 4–5.

Noam, E. *Im Altenheim Leben* (*Life in an Old Age Home*). Bonn: Eigenverlag des Deutschen Vereins fur Offentliche und Private Fürsorge, 1968.

Pastalan, L. A. "Privacy as an Expression of Human Territoriality." In Pastalan, L. A., and Carson, D. A. (eds.), *Spatial Behavior of Older People*. Ann Arbor: The University of Michigan, Institute of Gerontology, 1970.

Prochansky, H. M., Ittelson, W. H., and Rivlin, Leanne G. (eds.). *Environmental Psychology*. New York: Holt, Rinehart and Winston, 1970.

Shills, E. "Social Inquiry and the Autonomy of the Individual." In Lerner, D., *The Human Meaning of the Social Sciences*. Magnolia, Mass.: Peter Smith, 1959.

Townsend, P. *The Last Refuge: A Survey of Residential Institutions and Homes for the Aged in England and Wales*. London: Routledge and Kegan Paul, 1962, 352.

U.S. Department of Health, Education and Welfare. "Skilled Nursing Facilities." *Federal Register*, 1974, 39, No. 193, Part 2, October 3, 35775–76.

U.S. Department of Health, Education and Welfare. *Long-Term Care Facility Improvement Study*. Washington, D.C.: The Department, Public Health Service, Publication No. (OS) 76-500021, 1975, 62.

U.S. Department of Health, Education and Welfare, *Forward Plan for Health: FY 1978–82*. Washington, D.C.: The Department, Public Health Service, Publication No. (OS) 76-50046, 1976.

U.S. Senate Special Committee on Aging. Sub-committee on Long-Term Care. *Nursing Home Care in the United States: Failure in Public Policy: The Litany of Nursing Home Abuses and an Examination of the Roots of the Controversy*. Washington, D.C.: U.S. Government Printing Office, 1974.

Weinberg, J. "On Adding Insight to Injury." *Gerontologist*, 1976, 16, Part I, 4–10.

Chapter
11

Gerontological Occupations

It is difficult to estimate the total number of people employed in planning, developing, delivering, and evaluating services for older persons. The U.S. Department of Labor estimated that in 1976 over a million people were employed in occupations that were clearly defined as within the aging network and related systems (U.S. DOL, 1976). Those employed in area agencies on aging, state and federal units on aging, long-term care facilities, legal service programs, housing for older persons, senior adult education programs, and human service agencies for older persons were included.

It is apparent that the number of people employed in serving the elderly is growing and that more agencies are recognizing the desirability of having at least one aging specialist on their staffs. As mentioned in Chapter 1, not all agencies use the same definition of "older person." In addition, many employees serve clients of all ages and would not necessarily be identified as working in the field of aging. Thus, the Department of Labor statistics probably underestimated the number of people employed in aging service programs.

Academic Preparation for Working with Older Persons

Aging specialists are often referred to as gerontologists, but the definition of gerontologist is every bit as varied as the definition of older person. Broadly defined, *gerontology* is the study of aging and a *gerontologist* is one who studies aging. The terms "geriatrics" and "gerontology" are often interchanged, but *geriatrics* refers specifically to medical and rehabilitative aspects of aging, whereas gerontology is concerned with all aspects of aging. The term *social gerontology* "applies to the developmental and group behavior of adults following maturation and with the social phenomena which give rise to and rise out of the presence of older people in the population" (Tibbitts, 1964: 139). In addition to being the study of the process of aging and its interactions with society, social gerontology is concerned with identifying and ameliorating problems and needs of older persons and with increasing opportunities for the aged population's participation in society.

Most professionals identified with gerontology are members of a traditional profession or discipline such as social work, public administration, sociology, psychology, or biology. People in any of these fields may specialize in aging or gerontology. Thus, they may be described as gerontological social workers or gerontological psychologists rather than simply as gerontologists. Only recently have a few academic institutions begun to recognize gerontology as a field in itself—and there is still debate as to whether there really is such a field. Loeb contends that there is no such thing as the profession of gerontology, although one can " . . . be a gerontologist within most disciplines or professions" (1979: 34). On the other hand, Seltzer suggests, "We may not know *what* a gerontologist is, but we know *that* a gerontologist is" (1979: 38). While Seltzer agrees in part with Loeb's position that one must have training in one of the traditional disciplines before becoming a gerontological specialist, she believes that a body of cross-disciplinary knowledge and a set of professional beliefs exist and that these form the basis for the discipline of gerontology. Both authors agree that the ambiguity concerning what a gerontologist is and whether a gerontologist is, combined with the newness and rapid growth of the field, have contributed to the phenomenon of the "instant gerontologist." This term refers to the person without special preparation related to aging who either chooses to accept an opportunity to enter the aging field or is forced into the field by an administrative decision.

As recently as the late 1960s, the Department of Labor found that people responsible for social service delivery rarely received formal training in gerontology. The majority acquired gerontological knowledge and skills on the job (1976: 7).

Academic courses in gerontology began to proliferate in the 1960s and 1970s, following the 1961 and 1971 White House Conferences on Aging and the passage of the Older Americans Act of 1965. The focus of most academic programs, however, was on a basic profession or discipline with a core, specialization, or minor in aging or gerontology. That is, majors or degrees in gerontology were not developed, but courses in gerontology were offered to students majoring in fields such as social work, psychology, and sociology. In 1976, approximately 1200 institutions of higher learning were named by the Association for Gerontology in Higher Education as offering courses on aging. Only a few universities offered degrees in gerontology, and these were mainly in "applied gerontology" as opposed to research and education (Association for Gerontology in Higher Education, 1976).

The two subcategories of gerontology—research and education, and applied gerontology—have different goals and different training needs. *Applied gerontology*, as the label suggests, involves the planning, development, administration, and delivery of direct services. *Research and education* is concerned with theory, development of new knowledge, hypothesis testing through research, and teaching in institutions of higher learning.

Basic Disciplines in Research and Higher Education

The basic research-oriented academic disciplines associated with gerontology are biology, psychology, and sociology. There is general agreement that aging and the meaning of aging for the individual and society result from the interaction of biological, psychological, sociological, and environmental factors. Because research and higher education positions require in-depth training (usually at the Ph.D. level), few individuals are able to develop such skills in multiple disciplines. In addition to the obvious problems related to philosophies, frames of reference, and professional education, there is the question of time—it would require in the neighborhood of 20 years for a person to develop academic credentials in three or four disciplines. Thus, much of the theoretical and research work on aging is done by teams of gerontological biologists, gerontological psychologists, and gerontological sociologists. (This is not meant to suggest that other academic disciplines are not involved—only that these three are basic.) The terms "multidisciplinary" and "interdisciplinary" are often used in connection with such teams. *Interdisciplinary* usually connotes greater interaction or blending of disciplinary interests; *multidisciplinary* implies examination of the issues from several different points of view. Others involved in gerontological research include nutritionists, political scientists, nurses, social workers, and economists. The methods and concepts used in these fields are sometimes those of one or a combination of the three principal disciplines. For example, research by a nutritionist may involve biological, psychological, and sociological methods and concepts; research by a social worker is likely to involve concepts and methods from psychology and sociology.

Biological research in aging is primarily concerned with age-related changes in the chemical structure and the functioning of the cells, the organs, or the entire body. Such research may attempt to explain why hair turns gray, why supportive tissues lose elasticity, or why organ systems such as the circulatory system or the digestive system usually show a decline in functioning with age. Psychological research on aging is mostly concerned with age-related changes in sensory processes, memory, psychomotor responses, learning, concept formation, personality, and personal adjustment. Sociological research on aging usually concentrates on age-related changes in roles and relationships, the interplay between society and older persons, and the changing age composition of society (Atchley, 1980; Hendricks and Hendricks, 1981).

All of these research disciplines recognize and attempt to explain the wide diversity of older persons. For instance, researchers are trying to explain why some individuals experience severe physiological or psychological age-related decrements at a relatively early age while other individuals retain high levels of functioning into advanced age (Tibbitts, 1977; Atchley, 1980; Hendricks and Hendricks, 1981; Weg, 1975).

Applied Gerontology

Positions in applied gerontology may require preparation in a profession such as social work or public administration, with a speciality in aging. Other positions may not call for such preparation but instead require some understanding of several disciplines (Sterns et al., 1979). It is for jobs of this type that "generalist" degree programs in gerontology were developed. *Gerontology generalists* are well suited to positions requiring the ability to coordinate multiple professions. Some examples are director of a multipurpose senior center and director of an area agency on aging. The applied gerontology generalist has exposure to basic knowledge relating to the biology, psychology, sociology, and economics of aging, along with an overview of public administration, politics and social policy, planning, fiscal management, casework, counseling, and case management (Wilson, 1974). Obviously, the generalist does not acquire in-depth knowledge in all areas, but does acquire enough knowledge to communicate with members of each discipline, to comprehend the various frames of reference and concerns, and to approach the practical issues of aging with an understanding of the multifaceted nature of the aging process (Wilson, 1973; Elias, 1974).

Positions in Delivery of Services to the Aging

In 1979, the Administration on Aging in conjunction with the Bureau of Labor Statistics prepared a report on the personnel needs of state and local area agencies on aging. The report identified three major types of jobs that are found in all states and three additional types that are found in a substantial proportion of states. The major types are (1) directors of state and area agencies, who have general operational responsibility and who work with the political system, advocacy groups, and advisory groups; (2) program planners, who are responsible for developing state or area plans; and (3) program specialists, who are the intermediaries between state agencies and area agencies and between area agencies and service providers. Program specialists also provide technical assistance with program implementation and with the management of grants and contracts. Many agencies also employ (1) program executors, who provide direct service (such as advocates or lawyers); (2) training officers, who develop and implement in-service training for both agency staff and service providers in other agencies; and (3) researchers, who carry out evaluation studies on the effectiveness of services (U.S. DHEW, 1979a).

In the following discussion, occupations are grouped by typical agency job titles rather than by professional or disciplinary affiliation. Obviously, the two systems of classification overlap for occupations such as physician or nurse. Other positions (such as area agency director and planner) may be occupied by persons with training in any of several academic areas.

Social Workers

Social workers engage in a wide range of activities in the aging network. Rhones describes the role of social workers as helping people deal with their problems, but they do so in many different ways. Among the many subspecialities of social work are clinical social work, community organization, social policy and planning, and social services administration. At the master's degree level, most social workers are required to have some training in research and statistics (Rhones, 1976b).

Lowy suggests that the goal of social work is "to enable people . . . to carry out their social roles in a way that is consistent with their ego capacity" (1979: 45). Although the treatment component of social work is often stressed, there is increasing emphasis on prevention of problems as opposed to treating and "curing" people with problems. An additional focus of social work that has developed more recently is to improve the quality of life—to increase the client's opportunities for self-fulfillment. A social worker may provide casework for individuals and may assist the elderly in finding solutions for problems while developing coping capacities. A commonly used expression in social services is "helping clients to help themselves." Social workers also may become issue advocates, promoting political or social action to change conditions, thus preventing problems and increasing opportunities for self-development. Social workers who have specialized training in research and planning may be responsible for designing and implementing needs assessments and program evaluations and for developing service plans. Other workers may have primary responsibility for the administration of a service delivery agency or system (U.S. DHEW, 1979b).

Planners

A detailed description of the functions of planners appears in Chapter 3. Planners may have academic backgrounds in sociology, interdisciplinary planning, applied social gerontology, social work, public administration, business, or economics. Regardless of the academic field, planners must have basic skills in needs assessment research, evaluation research, and community organization, as well as knowledge of service delivery systems, budgeting, cost-benefit analysis, and communication. Planners must know how to locate, analyze, and interpret statistical data from a variety of sources and to formulate a rationale for setting priorities.

Monitors and Evaluators

Monitors and evaluators are usually employed in agencies responsible for planning and/or funding service delivery programs. Examples of such agencies are state units on aging, area agencies on aging, United Way agencies, and state human service agencies. Job duties include reviewing the progress made by service providers, reviewing budget reports, conducting evaluations of program process and impact, assisting in program development, and interpreting regulations for service providers. The academic preparation of monitors and evaluators is varied, but it generally parallels that of planners (U.S. DHEW, 1979a).

Advocates

People who assist in advancing the interests of either a single individual or a client group (personal advocacy) or of a particular cause (issue advocacy) are called advocates. They may be lay volunteers or higher trained professionals. In some agencies, the person designated as an advocate may have a law degree or a master's degree in social work. In other agencies, the advocate may be indigenous to the target population and have no academic preparation for the advocacy function. Lay persons who are known and trusted in particular target groups are often recruited and provided with on-the-job training in advocacy skills. These people have proven to be especially effective in working with minorities or with other potentially alienated groups.

Directors of State or Area Agencies on Aging

The state or area agency director needs to be knowledgeable about the political system and legislative processes; current legislation, rules, and regulations; the field of aging and the aging process; funding sources; and community organization. In addition, the director must have skills in public relations, communication, leadership, and administration (U.S. DHEW, 1979a). Although area agency director positions usually require a master's degree in a social service or administrative area, they are often filled through political appointments (Estes, 1979). The Administration on Aging has made efforts to educate local elected officials on the importance of having dedicated and well-qualified persons in these capacities. Since many of the positions have been filled with people who have demonstrated administrative ability but have no background in aging, in-service training programs, conferences, and workshops have been used to provide gerontological knowledge (U.S. DHEW, 1979a). (Figure 11.1 duplicates a job description for an area agency director.) While some differences in specific requirements and activities may exist, most of the approximately 700 area agencies in the United States have similar descriptions for the position of director.

Administrators of Nursing Homes, Housing Programs, and Senior Centers

All administrators need basic management skills covering fiscal, personnel, and physical plant management. In addition, they must have knowledge of the aging process and of characteristics of older people. Differences lie in the nature and goals of the setting in which they serve and in the types of older persons being served. Nursing homes care for a more dependent, less healthy, and more physically

Figure 11.1 Job Description: Area Agency Director

I. *GENERAL*:
    The Director of the Area Agency on Aging of the _____
    Regional Planning Council has overall responsibility for man-
    agement of all mandated activities of the Agency, including
    compliance with all elements of the annual Plan of Action
    (PoA) and grant/contract award. The Director is supervised
    directly by the Executive Director of the _____ Regional
    Planning Council.

II. *RESPONSIBILITIES*:
    The Area Agency on Aging Director has responsibility for
    activity in the following areas:
    1. Coordination and direction of staff efforts in development
        and administration of the area Plan of Action (PoA).
    2. Development and coordination of potential or available
        and untapped resources appropriate to the aging network
        whether public or private.
    3. Ensure coordination and cooperation of funded service
        delivery programs to achieve maximum cost effective
        performance.
    4. Provision of leadership and advocacy activities in all areas
        of effort in the community of older Americans.
    5. Oversight of fiscal responsibilities of the Area Agency in
        support of the Plan of Action and all of its components.
    6. Conduct of all programs and activities of the Agency in a
        manner consonant with the advice of the Area Agency on
        Aging's Citizen Advisory Council (CAC).
    7. Liaison with the Florida Department of Health and Reha-
        bilitative Services at the District and State level.
    8. General oversight of all technical assistance provided to
        grantees or potential grantees.

III. *MINIMUM TRAINING AND EXPERIENCE*:
    A master's degree from an accredited college or university in
    public administration, sociology, psychology, gerontology,
    public health, planning, business administration or a related
    academic area and a minimum of three years of administrative
    and supervisory experience to include extensive experience in
    project management and/or community organization and
    planning. Any exceptions to the degree requirements must be
    cleared through the District Program Office and approved by
    the Aging and Adult Services State Program Office Director.

Note: This is an actual job description contained in a Florida area plan and
circulated for recruiting a director in 1981.

and mentally impaired older population than do either housing programs or senior centers. The latter two serve all types of elderly, but mainly those who are ambulatory, relatively active, and largely independent (U.S. DOL, 1976).

Although most nursing home administrators are not clinical health professionals, they must understand health problems and health care delivery to a greater extent than must housing or senior center directors. Nursing home administrators are licensed; they must pass an examination in addition to meeting the educational requirements set by each state. Continuing education in appropriate areas is required for nursing home administrators so that they can keep up with new developments in management, health care, financing, public policy, and legislation. Specific requirements for licensing of nursing home administrators vary from state to state, but the trend is toward greater uniformity and higher standards (U.S. DHEW, 1980).

The need for specialized managers for housing for the elderly has been recognized only since the 1960s. The traditional housing administrator is concerned mainly with maintenance of the facility and with financial management. He or she must have some knowledge of maintenance of equipment (heating and cooling systems, plumbing, appliances) and must be able to keep records and handle monetary receipts and disbursements. If applicable to the project, the manager may have to be acquainted with federal, state, or local regulations. The specialist in housing for the elderly must have these abilities plus an understanding of the aging process and the resources available to meet social and health needs of older persons. The housing administrator may arrange for and administer the delivery of social services to residents of the facility and often serves as an adviser or information-and-referral source for residents (International Center for Social Gerontology, 1979).

Senior center directors usually are responsible for budgeting, preparation of project proposals, and program reporting and evaluation, as well as for the day-to-day activities of the center. In a large center, the director may supervise a number of professional staff members, including social workers, adult educators, nutritionists, and recreation specialists. In a small center, the director may carry out the functions of such specialists or arrange for their services on a consultative or part-time basis. Senior center directors must be well informed about the full range of social services for older persons, social policy and legislation, funding sources, and community organizations. Academic preparation usually includes a bachelor's degree and often a master's degree in public administration, social work, social science, business administration, or gerontology. If the director does not have a degree or specialization in gerontology, additional courses, workshops, and in-service training in gerontology are essential (U.S. DOL, 1976; Birren, 1971).

Gerontological Recreation Specialists

There are two subspecialties—community recreation and therapeutic recreation—for gerontological recreation specialists. The *community recreation specialist* may work in a senior center, a city or county recreation program, or a voluntary agency that provides recreational activities for active, nonimpaired older persons. The *therapeutic recreation specialist* would most likely be employed in a nursing home, a chronic disease hospital, or a home health program and would be more concerned with specialized recreation for impaired older persons. Both types of recreation workers need to be knowledgeable about the aging process, characteristics of older persons, community resources, health problems of aging, and first aid. In terms of academic background, an associate (community college) degree in recreation with specialized courses in gerontology is the bare minimum. Most positions call for at least a bachelor's degree; those positions with major program planning, development, and administrative responsibilities generally require a master's degree with either a specialization or a major in gerontology (U.S. DOL, 1979c).

Specialists in Health-Related Professions

Essentially all of the health-related professions have specialists who work with older persons. As the very old segment of the population continues to grow, needs for these specialists can be expected to increase. Positions exist in both private and public sectors and in institutional and community settings. Professional workers in fields such as nursing, physical therapy, occupational therapy, medical social work, and dietetics must complete a prescribed course of study and meet certification or licensing requirements of the profession. These workers may then specialize in working with older persons through taking additional courses and on-the-job training. Most professional schools require at least a brief module on aging for all students. Although this sometimes stimulates interest in specializing in this area, it often has the reverse effect. That is, instructors are frequently misinformed or uninformed about the positive aspects of aging and present a negative view that discourages students from selecting careers in aging. This situation is changing;

the positive aspects of working with the elderly are being included in more health training programs.

Physicians and Dentists

Historically, study of the special needs of the aged has been neglected in the training of physicians and dentists. An outspoken critic of this neglect is Robert Butler, the first director of the National Institute on Aging. Butler commented: "One study of University of California medical students showed that their attitudes towards old people actually deteriorated over the course of their four years in medical school. Medical students were not exposed to healthy older people in the same fashion that they are exposed to healthy babies in sunny, well-baby nurseries and clinics" (1978: 7). In a later report, Butler stated: "In order to effectively meet the needs of older people for high quality medical treatment—accurate diagnosis, sensitive care, and effective treatment—it is imperative that the special perspectives of the particular body of knowledge known as 'geriatric medicine' be introduced into the curriculum of our 114 medical schools . . ." (1979: 1).

The National Institute on Aging (NIA) has used several approaches to stimulate interest in geriatric medicine and geriatric dentistry in recent years. Studies and demonstrations have been conducted on ways to incorporate content on aging in medical training. NIA has provided seed money for research and teaching, has conducted numerous conferences, and has worked with major professional associations including the National Academy of Sciences, the American Medical Student Association, the Association of Professors of Medicine, and the National Institute of Dental Research. Thanks in large part to the efforts of the NIA, professional schools and associations are devoting increasing attention to training on the special characteristics and needs of older adults.

Advisory Council Members

Most human service delivery programs include community advisory councils. These councils are generally made up of a cross-section of persons knowledgeable about the community, its people, and its resources. Some agencies and some funding sources require that a majority of the advisory council members be consumers of the agency's services. Other agencies demand representation from particular subgroups, such as ethnic or racial minorities. Although the position of advisory council member is not an occupation in the usual sense, it is extremely important in the development and delivery of services. Advisory council members can enhance the applicability and acceptability of human services by pointing out certain actions to be taken or avoided, by advising service providers and planners of problems and solutions, and by legitimizing the agency program to the target community (U.S. DOL, 1976; Gray Panthers, 1980; Collins and Mills, 1979).

Summary

This chapter covers the emerging field of gerontology. Most people working in research and higher education on aging have been trained in a basic discipline or profession such as biology, sociology, psychology, social work, or public administration. Training in gerontology is added to create a gerontological psychologist, gerontological social worker, and so on. The rapid growth of gerontology, combined with the ambiguity of who or what a gerontologist is, has given rise to the phenomenon of the "instant gerontologist." This is someone who, for a variety of reasons, is declared to be a gerontologist. As the field matures, however, a body of knowledge, professional beliefs, and ethics is emerging to constitute the core of what might be called the academic discipline of gerontology.

The principal academic disciplines involved in research and training on aging, biology, psychology, and sociology, have been reviewed briefly, and the differences in training for research and teaching versus training for applied gerontology have been described. Selected categories of occupations in service delivery were discussed in terms of functions and academic preparation. Positions such as housing administrator, senior center director, and planner may be filled by persons having any of several academic majors, including management, public administration, social work, sociology, and gerontology. The intent of this chapter has been to provide a brief overview of the occupational categories most often involved in work with older people. Additional information elsewhere in this volume describes the activities of people providing specific services such as information and referral, planning, and health care. There are some occupational categories in which people work only with the elderly, but most jobs are likely to involve work with other age groups as well.

Opportunities for specialists in aging are increasing in a wide range of occupations. Certain job categories may experience short-term decreases because of political policy variances and changes in public fund appropriations. Demographic trends and the development of products and services directed toward the elderly suggest there will be a growing need for gerontological specialists, however.

References

Association for Gerontology in Higher Education. *National Directory of Education Programs in Gerontology*. Madison, WI: McBeath Institute on Aging and Adult Life, 1976.

Atchley, R. C. *The Social Forces in Later Life*, 3rd ed. Belmont, CA: Wadsworth Publishing Co., 1980.

Beattie, W. M., Jr. "Aging and the Social Services." In *Handbook of Aging and the Social Sciences*, eds. R. H. Binstock and E. Shanas, pp. 619–642. New York: Van Nostrand Reinhold Co., 1976.

Birren, J. E. *Training: Background and Issues*. Washington, D.C.: White House Conference on Aging, 1971.

Birren, J. E., and I. S. Hirschfield. "The Experience of Gerontology in Higher Education in America." In *Gerontology in Higher Education*, eds. H. L. Sterns et al., pp. 2–13. Belmont, CA: Wadsworth Publishing Co., 1979.

Butler, R. N. *Thoughts on Geriatric Medicine*. Washington, D.C.: National Institute on Aging, 1978.

_____. *Special Report on Aging: 1979*. Washington, D.C.: National Institute on Aging, 1979.

Collins, M. A., and J. E. Mills. *Boards and Advisory Councils: A Key to Effective Management*. Washington, D.C.: The National Council on the Aging, 1979.

Elias, M. "Symposium—The Real World and the Ivory Tower." *The Gerontologist* 14 (1974): 525–526.

Estes, C. *The Aging Enterprise*. San Francisco: Springer Publishing Co., 1979.

Gray Panthers, *The Gray Panther Manual, Vol. II*. Philadelphia, PA: Gray Panthers, 1980.

Harbert, A. S., and L. H. Ginsberg. *Human Servies for Older Adults: Concepts and Skills*. Belmont, CA: Wadsworth Publishing Co., 1979.

Hendricks, J., and C. D. Hendricks. *Aging in Mass Society*, 2nd ed. Cambridge, MA: Winthrop Publishers, 1981.

International Center for Social Gerontology. *A Book of Readings for Use in the ICSG Technical Assistance Project on Housing and Services for Older Adults*. Washington, D.C.: International Center for Social Gerontology, 1979.

Loeb, M. B. "Gerontology Is Not a Profession—The Oldest or the Youngest." In *Gerontology in Higher Education*, eds. H. L. Sterns et al., pp. 34–36. Belmont, CA: Wadsworth Publishing Co., 1979.

Lowy, L. *Social Work with the Aging*. New York: Harper and Row, 1979.

National Institute on Aging. *Special Report on Aging 1980*. Washington, D.C.: U.S. Government Printing Office, 1980.

Rhones, P. L. "Recreation Occupations." In *Occupational Outlook Quarterly Special Issue: Working with Older People*, pp. 49–53. Washington, D.C.: U.S. Government Printing Office, Fall, 1976a.

_____. "Social Work." In *Occupational Outlook Quarterly Special Issue: Working with Older People*, pp. 45–49. Washington, D.C.: U.S. Government Printing Office, Fall, 1976b.

Seltzer, M. "Reflections on the Phenomenon of the Instant Gerontologist." In *Gerontology in Higher Education*, eds. H. L. Sterns et al., pp. 37–40. Belmont, CA: Wadsworth Publishing Co., 1979.

Sterns, H. L., E. F. Ansello, B. M. Sprouse, and R. Layfield-Faux, eds. *Gerontology in Higher Education: Developing Institutional and Community Strength.* Belmont, CA: Wadsworth Publishing Co., 1979.

Tibbitts, C. "The Future of Research in Social Gerontology." In *Age with a Future*, ed. P. FromHausen, pp. 139–145. Copenhagen: Munksgaard Publishers, 1964.

_____. "Introduction." In *Ethical Considerations in Long Term Care*, eds. W. E. Winston and A. J. E. Wilson III, pp. 1–16. St. Petersburg, FL: Eckerd College Gerontology Center, 1977.

U.S. Department of Health, Education and Welfare, Administration on Aging. *Employment Issues in Agencies on Aging.* Occasional Papers in Gerontology. Washington, D.C.: U.S. Government Printing Office, 1979a.

_____, Administration on Aging. *Employment Issues in Social Work with the Elderly.* Occasional Papers in Gerontology. Washington, D.C.: U.S. Government Printing Office, 1979b.

_____, Administration on Aging. *Human Resource Issues in the Field of Aging: The Nursing Home Industry* (revised). Occasional Papers in Gerontology. Washington, D.C.: U.S. Government Printing Office, 1980.

U.S. Department of Labor. *Occupational Outlook Quarterly Special Issue: Working with Older People.* Washington, D.C.: U.S. Government Printing Office, Fall, 1976.

_____, Bureau of Labor Statistics. *Nurses Who Work with Older People.* Washington, D.C.: U.S. Government Printing Office, 1979a.

_____, Bureau of Labor Statistics. *Nursing Home Administrators Who Care for Older People.* Washington, D.C.: U.S. Government Printing Office, 1979b.

_____, Bureau of Labor Statistics. *Recreation Workers Who Organize Activities for Older People.* Washington, D.C.: U.S. Government Printing Office, 1979c.

Weg, R. "Concepts in Education and Training for Gerontology: New Career Patterns." *The Gerontologist* 13 (1973): 449–452.

_____. "Changing Physiology of Aging: Normal and Pathological." In *Aging: Scientific Perspectives and Social Issues*, eds. D. S. Woodruff and J. E. Birren, pp. 229–256. New York: D. Van Nostrand Co., 1975.

_____. "Ethical Issues in Training." In *Ethical Considerations in Long Term Care*, eds. W. E. Winston and A. J. E. Wilson III, pp. 171–184. St. Petersburg, FL: Eckerd College Gerontology Center, 1977.

Wilson, A. J. E., III. "Statement on Training Needs in Gerontology." In *Training Needs in Gerontology: Hearings Before the Special Committee on Aging*, Part 1, pp. 9–14. Washington, D.C.: U.S. Government Printing Office, 1973.

_____. "Response to Training for Trainers." *The Gerontologist* 14 (1974): 536–537.

Glossary

Administration on Aging (AoA): The federal agency established to carry out the provisions of the Older Americans Act.

Advocacy services: Arguing for or presenting another's cause. Advocacy may be personal (for an individual), or it may relate to an issue affecting large numbers or classes of individuals.

Age dependency ratio: The ratio of persons below the usual working ages (under 18) and above the usual working ages (65 and over) to those of working age (18 through 64).

Ageism: Prejudice and discrimination directed toward persons who have achieved a chronological age defined as "old."

Area agency on aging (AAA): A local agency designated by the state unit on aging. The AAA is responsible for developing and carrying out an area plan in accordance with the Older Americans Act.

Chronological age: Age measured in terms of the length of time (usually in years) since a person's birth.

Cohort: A group of people having some common characteristic. This term is frequently used with reference to a group of people born in the same year or during a specified time period.

Comprehensive and coordinated system: A system providing all needed supportive services in an efficient manner with a minimum of duplication (1981 Older Americans Act definition).

Continuum of services: A full range of preventive, supportive, and restorative services.

Deinstitutionalization movement: Concerted efforts to avoid placing persons in institutions such as mental hospitals and to remove those so placed. The movement emphasizes development of support systems in communities as a substitute for institutionalization.

Dependency: A physical, mental, social, or economic state in which a person must rely on others for assistance on a regular basis.

Disregard: Certain income or resources that are exempted when a person's eligibility for programs is being determined through a means test.

Functional age: Age based on capacity to perform rather than on simple chronological age. Functional age may be measured in multiple areas (such as sociological, physiological, and so on).

Incidence: The number of *new* cases of a disease or condition that occur over a specified period of time, usually expressed as a rate.

Indirect income (also called in-kind income): Goods and services provided without cost or at reduced cost, such as free medical care, rent supplements, or senior citizen discounts.

Life expectancy: The average number of years a person can expect to live if current age-specific death rates remain constant. Life expectancy may be expressed at birth or at any given year of age.

Long-term care: A range of services (including medical, nursing, rehabilitative, casework, and supportive) that is provided in either institutional or noninstitutional settings and is expected to be provided for a relatively long time.

Means test: Limitations of financial resources (income and assets) as stipulated in eligibility standards for financial aid or social services.

Medicare: A national health insurance program for all persons who either are age 65 and over or are totally and permanently disabled. It is authorized through Title XVIII of the Social Security Act.

Medicaid: A combined federal-state system to pay for health care for the poor of all ages. It is authorized through Title XIX of the Social Security Act.

Morbidity: Any departure from "good" health, usually used in reference to rates of illness and impairment.

Needs assessment: The process of gathering information from multiple sources to estimate the nature and extent of needs for intervention or services.

Older Americans Act: Basic federal legislation providing for the establishment of a network of federal, state, and local agencies to carry out planning, coordination, service delivery, research and demonstration, training, and other activities authorized by the act.

Planning and service area (PSA): A substate geographic area designated by the state unit on aging for purposes of planning under the provisions of the Older Americans Act.

Prevalence: The number of cases of a disease or condition that exist at one point in time, usually expressed as a rate.

Protective services: A full range of casework and supportive services provided for clients who may be incapable of exercising sound judgment and who have no personal social support system.

Replacement ratio (income): The ratio of income immediately after retirement to income during the period just prior to retirement.

State unit on aging (SUA): The unit of state government designated to administer Older Americans Act programs at the state level.

Supplemental Security Income (SSI): A national program guaranteeing a minimum income to older persons who meet a restrictive means test.

Title XX: A title of the Social Security Act that provides for programs of social services for poor and nearly poor persons to be administered by the states.

Index